MORE THAN
YORKSHIRE PUDDINGS

FOOD, STORIES AND OVER 100 RECIPES FROM GOD'S OWN COUNTY

ELAINE LEMM

GREAT NORTHERN

Great Northern Books
PO Box 1380, Bradford, BD5 5FB
www.greatnorthernbooks.co.uk

ISBN: 978-1-912101-46-7

Design and layout: David Burrill

Photo credits:
All images © Elaine Lemm
except
page 99, British Asparagus
page 108, Illiya Vjestica
page 169, Julia Gartland – Food52

CIP Data
A catalogue for this book is available from the British Library

Elaine Lemm is a former chef and cookery school owner and for over 20 years a freelance food and recipe writer.

As well as seven years as Food and Wine Editor at *Yorkshire Life* magazine, Elaine has written for many leading magazines including *Waitrose Food Illustrated*, *National Geographic Food*, *Olive* and *BBC Good Food* magazines and has an enviable job as restaurant critic for the *Yorkshire Post*.

For 14 years Elaine wrote and developed recipes for the New York Times Company, later called Spruce Eats, which is one of the leading food sites in the world. Elaine is also the author of three food books including the acclaimed *Great Book of Yorkshire Pudding* which sells worldwide and is in its third Edition.

She works remotely from her home in North Yorkshire, where she lives with her husband and occasionally has a house full of kids and family to feed, which she loves. For downtime, Elaine enjoys yoga, is a keen sculptor and when she has time, loves nothing more than pottering about in the garden and long walks in the glorious Yorkshire landscape.

Contents

Preface

I am often asked about this book's title, which has changed many times during its writing, having somehow never seemed to capture its intention. Then, as can often happen, there was a moment when it came to me. To explain why and how I must go back a few years to when I first approached my publishers Great Northern with a book proposal.

I had felt for a long time that, no matter where I was in the world, if I mentioned I came from Yorkshire, I was asked about Yorkshire puddings.

I would, of course, extol their virtues, they are loved and are an intrinsic part of our culinary heritage, but I often found myself defending all the other fabulous food produced, grown and cooked here.

"I want people to know that Yorkshire is more than Yorkshire puddings," I told Great Northern, "that there is so much more here than the puds!"

However, after much deliberation, the owners said no, and that was that.

Six months or so later, they rang me. Though they felt the same about my book proposal, they did believe a book about Yorkshire puddings had legs. So, the *Great Book of Yorkshire Puddings* came about and was true to their predictions and has been universally popular and now in its third edition. I am fiercely proud of that little book, one that keeps giving and has taken me onto national and international television, radio, endless interviews and emails and messages, now possibly in their thousands, thanking me for the book.

There followed two more, *The Great Book of Rhubarb* and *The Great Book of Tea*, and though successful, they never came close to the love of the first.

Time moved on, and Yorkshire's prominence in the world's eyes has grown exponentially in recent years due to many factors. Following a change of ownership at Great Northern, the earlier proposal was looked at again, and this time got the green light. Though a small thing called a global pandemic delayed the book for some time, here it is.

This book is not a history of Yorkshire food, which has been handled so well by writer Peter Brears in his book *Traditional Food in Yorkshire*, or a cookbook packed with the legacy recipes we all know so well – though there are, of course, some of our favourites in here. Instead, it is a book highlighting the breadth of what is available here in recipes influenced by the countries I have lived and worked in and the people I have met along the way. But above all, it is a book to show that Yorkshire truly is more than Yorkshire puddings.

Yorkshire Food

Yorkshire is famous for so many foods from rhubarb to Wensleydale cheese, Pontefract cakes, fat rascals, chocolate and confectionery in abundance, and of course, Yorkshire puddings. But it is so much more thanks to its dramatic coastline, rivers, rolling hills and the 680 square miles of Yorkshire dales. There are the moors, wolds, and the industrial belt across west and into south Yorkshire, which altogether make up England's largest county and one of the nation's largest producers of food.

From meat, fish and seafood, bakery, fruits and vegetables, grains, herbs and dairy, large producers and small artisans, there's a bit of everything; even if it is not grown or reared in the county, one of the fabulous farm shops, delis, food halls and independent shops will sell it.

So, undeniably, a culinary journey through Yorkshire is absurdly delicious, exciting and immensely varied. Expect to have your senses assaulted with an untold number of tastes, scents, textures on a voyage rich with many much-loved traditional foods through to the inventive creations of trailblazing chefs and dishes from or influenced by most cuisines around the world. The county also has over 7,000 places to eat and drink, from pubs, cafés and tearooms to Michelin-starred restaurants and everything in between. No other area outside London has as many highly recommended places to dine listed in leading food guides.

Is it any wonder it is called God's Own County?

Nanny Lemm circa 1940s

Intro

I have read so many cookbook introductions reflecting on childhoods filled with holidays – or even homes – in idyllic locations like Tuscany and Provence. Places that so easily inspire the desire to cook, write or work with food. My childhood had none of those influences, yet by a circuitous route, I ended up working and living in many of those beautiful places and more.

I am a Leeds lass. I was born in Armley, though my mum always made us laugh by adding, "Upper Armley, not near the jail", whenever anyone asked where we lived. I am the second eldest of seven, and our house was quite literally a madhouse with all of us, plus dogs, cats, the tortoise, and endless rounds of friends in and out. It is only now, as I am older, that I often wonder how on earth my parents managed with such a brood, but they did. We all "turned out alright", as we say here in Yorkshire, and I hope we continue to make them proud today with our own families, children and grandchildren.

Food was, of course, hugely central to our family life and Mum cooked from scratch almost every day even though back then we had a two-course cooked lunch at school. Dad was also a good cook though he much preferred growing the food and was a great gardener, a love he also passed on to us. The cooking and gardening, I believe, came from his mum, my Nanny Lemm who also had some impact on me.

Nanny had begun her life in service at one of the stately piles in Yorkshire. She remarkably went from scullery maid to head cook, which was rare. She came out of service when she married. I never knew my grandad, because they had divorced, but I remember my lovely bear of a step-grandad, Uncle Ted, and going to their house, and my first ever food memory was her cooking the most amazing Yorkshire puddings.

Having passed my eleven-plus exam, I went to West Leeds Girls High School, a grammar school that was academic and strict, and there were three pivotal moments there that essentially set me on paths I had never thought possible.

The first was winning a bursary awarded annually for 'deserving' pupils; for those who would benefit but could not afford some activity or school trip. There was an educational cruise to the Eastern Mediterranean, and though my friends Susan, Janice and Katy were going, I had not even mentioned it at home. I was awarded the annual bursary for the trip, and it changed me forever. We flew to Venice, boarded the ship and went on to visit Corfu, Israel, Cyprus and Athens. We had such adventures, fun and some learning on the way, and my lifelong love of travel was born.

The second was a three-week French exchange to Marseille in our 'O' level year of French conversation. My love of French food and language came from that experience. And finally, when it came to my elective 'O' levels, I could not decide between art or domestic science. I loved both. Miss Kingston, my domestic science teacher, even went to see my mother, insisting I take her subject. So I did, yet I will always be thankful to Mrs Fair, who, when I returned to art in the sixth form, worked so hard with me and helped me get my place at Leeds College of Art, where I studied fashion and textiles. From that, my love of all things art, especially sculpture, is still as strong today, and it is also where I met my lifelong friend Mandi.

For the next 12 years, food was no longer my focus. Though I enjoyed working in fashion, it was never a passion. So I went from designing to teaching; came out of a disastrous marriage and, by a route I will save for another book, lived and worked in the US, Mexico, Scandinavia, and eventually in France. And that was when everything changed.

My then partner and I had a lovely home in rural France, acres of land, a beautiful vegetable garden, fruit trees, and eventually ducks, geese, hens, four sheep and two dogs; I was in heaven. I had time to explore and loved going to the markets and discovering new foods, enchanted by the seasonality of the food we grew and could buy. My passion for food was back – big time. There was so much that reminded me of how, when growing up, our food had been intrinsic to family life; those values were evident in rural France, where cooking and caring for the family were so important.

I could devote a whole book to my years living there, of the fun of sharing it, especially with my best friend Yvonne, who stayed with us for extended periods; we had such fun together figuring everything out. I also met the gorgeous 80-year-old Mme. Grande who taught me so much about French cooking, and you will find her popping up through the recipes here in the book. After that, I changed direction and went to Paris to the Ritz-Escoffier school for some classical training, but I mainly taught myself along with Mme. Grande's help and asking questions of anyone locally I could; the French are so willing to share their love of food.

It was also in France where I eventually started teaching others to cook. I so enjoy sharing the joy of food, and what an environment to do it in. Yvonne and I set up the classes together, which was a huge success. The local French often expressed their thoughts on two English women audacious enough to teach French cuisine, but it was always said with a wry smile. Eventually, my time in France ended with the breakdown of my relationship. I was distraught, but I headed home to Yorkshire, to family and friends who helped me through.

Life moved on, and I set up the Cuisine Éclairée cooking school. Yvonne and I started it in Yorkshire, then on to residential holidays at Villa Caturgelio in Tuscany, where my sister Liz joined the team. With the help of my wonderful Swedish friend Lena, I taught weekend courses at the renowned Franska Matsalen restaurant at the Grand Hotel in Stockholm and occasionally headed to New Orleans to teach as well. It was hard but excellent work, which I remember with such fondness.

Around this time, I started writing for the *Yorkshire Post*. I had opened my restaurant in North Yorkshire and was teaching less and less, and sharing my work through writing took over. Eventually, I sold the restaurant and, at the same time, was offered a job as Food and Wine Editor at the prestigious *Yorkshire Life* magazine, where, on my first ever commission, I met – and later married – my wonderful husband. He was the assigned photographer that day. I became stepmum to his three children, Emma, Lucy and Josh, and my life became rich and fulfilling in a very different way, especially now with our three beautiful grandchildren.

Though I still occasionally teach, I am more often now at my desk writing, in the kitchen developing recipes for magazines and websites, out reviewing restaurants, and chairing and judging local and national awards. I am, though, always at my happiest when I am creating food and sharing it with others. So, I hope you like the eclectic mix of recipes in this book born out of all those experiences I have been fortunate to have had and through my never-ending love of Yorkshire and the wealth of food it has to offer.

Mum and Dad 1954

How to Cook from this Book

All the recipes in this book are intended to be cooked at home, to share with family and friends, and many are ones I cook regularly. They are not cheffy, and most are not overly complicated, though there are a few for those who like a bit of a challenge.

The emphasis in all the recipes is the ingredients, almost all of which will be available in Yorkshire, either made, grown or bred here and indeed on sale in one or other of the many supermarkets, delis, food halls and farm shops. You can see a list of my favourite suppliers on page 196. None of the recipes is dependent on you buying what you need in or from Yorkshire. I am supremely proud of what we have here, but use what you have and what is available to you.

Where you can, seek out your local butcher, fish and cheesemongers and independent shops. I am not against supermarkets, but the success of these small businesses is dependent on our custom. Service from an independent is often more personal, and in my experience, the specialists I meet are always willing to share their knowledge if you ask.

A Few Notes on Ingredients

Eggs:
I do not state the size of eggs to use in most of the recipes unless it is imperative. I always used large eggs until the lovely Yolk Farm at Minskip, who raise the happiest hens with the most delicious eggs, pointed out that they are hard for the hens to lay. Also, mixing egg sizes is better not just for the hens but also for the producer. And as consumers, we also benefit as the smaller eggs have more yolk and better whites. I have barely noticed a difference in my cooking since using them.

Flour is always plain, and butter unsalted unless stated otherwise.

Measures are metric with weights in grams and kilos. Volume uses tea and tablespoons, millilitres and litres. There's a handy conversion table below for those who use imperial.

Oven temperatures are for a fan oven. If using without, raise the temperature by around 20°C.

Equipment

I am so lucky to have many time-and-effort-saving gadgets in my kitchen, things I have gathered together over the years. I have kept these to a minimum in the recipes, suggesting where you can use one or an alternative.

If you prefer to use a pressure or slow cooker, a microwave, or anything else that works for you, go for it. Personally, I would be lost without my Thermomix or my recent new kitchen friend, an electric Sage multicooker which I use almost daily. Still, I have not included these in any recipes.

However, the equipment most essential for me in the kitchen is my knives, which are over 20 years old. I have an eclectic mix of knives bought while travelling or given to me to try, but I end up using only my 24 cm chef knife, a flexible filleting knife, a small paring one for vegetables, plus my lovely old bread knife.

Above all, as a food writer, I hope you enjoy the recipes and make them your own in any way you wish.

All the recipes in the book are written using metric measurements. Personally, I find having too many measurements in the ingredients list with grams, then ounces, then cups can become confusing. I have therefore stuck to the one I use all the time and here is a quick conversion table to help.

For US cups which vary in volume depending on what you are using, there are several great online sources for quick conversions.

WEIGHT	VOLUME	MEASUREMENTS	CELSIUS	FAHRENHEIT	GAS MARK
10g	¼oz	1.25ml	¼tsp	3mm	⅛in	110°C	225°F	¼
15g	½oz	2.5ml	½tsp	5mm	¼in	120°C	250°F	½
25g	1oz	5ml	1tsp	1cm	½in	140°C	275°F	1
50g	1¾oz	30ml	1fl oz	2cm	¾in	150°C	300°F	2
75g	2¾oz	50ml	2fl oz	2.5cm	1in	160°C	320°F	3
100g	3½oz	100ml	3½fl oz	3cm	1¼in	180°C	350°F	4
150g	5½oz	150ml	5fl oz	¼ pint	4cm	1½in	190°C	375°F	5
175g	6oz	200ml	7fl oz	⅓ pint	5cm	2in	200°C	400°F	6
200g	7oz	300ml	10 fl oz	½ pint	6cm	2 1½in	220°C	425°F	7
225g	8oz	500ml	18fl oz	7cm	2¾in	230°C	455°F	8
250g	9oz	600ml	20fl oz	1 pint	8cm	3¼in			
275g	9¾oz	700ml	1¼ pints	9cm	3½in			
300g	10½oz	850ml	1 ½ pints	10mm	4in			
350g	12oz	1L	1¾ pints	12cm	4 1½in			
375g	13oz	1.2L	2 pints	15cm	6in			
400g	14oz		17cm	6½in			
425g	15oz		18cm	7in			
450g	1lb		20cm	8in			
500g	1lb 2oz		23cm	9in			
700g	1½lb		24cm	9½in			
750g	1lb 10oz		25cm	10in			
1kg	2¼oz		30cm	12in			
1.25kg	2lb 12oz					
1.5kg	3lb 5oz					
2kg	4½lb					
2.25kg	5lb					
2.5kg	5½lb					
3kg	6½lb					

LEGACY RECIPES

Perfect Yorkshire Puddings – Every Time

Despite my plea that Yorkshire food is more than its famous puddings, to leave out a recipe for them would be a shame, so here is mine.

When I was researching the *Great Book of Yorkshire Pudding*, most of my work was trying to uncover the true origin of why they are called after the county, plus a definitive recipe. Unfortunately, I failed with the former; however, with the latter, after interviewing countless chefs, family, friends and even strangers, I concluded that everyone, it seems, has their own recipe that works for them, which is terrific.

For those who don't, though, here is my recipe. It isn't the method my mother showed me, as she had the knack of making amazing puddings without measuring anything. Instead, it is one I have developed over the years to produce perfect puddings every time, and I have lost count of the number of emails, letters, and photographs from across the globe after being published in the book and online, showing off their successes.

So, if you have a recipe and it works for you, go for it. If not, then try this. It does work, and the key to it is whatever quantity of eggs you use, use an equal amount of milk and of flour; it really is that simple.

serves 6

4 fresh eggs, measured in a jug
equal quantity of milk to eggs
pinch of salt
equal quantity of plain flour to eggs
lard, beef dripping or vegetable oil for cooking

1. Pour the eggs and milk into a large mixing bowl, add the pinch of salt and whisk thoroughly with an electric or hand whisk until foamy. Leave to stand for about 10 minutes to allow the bubbles to subside.

2. Sieve the flour into the milk and egg mixture and beat again using an electric or hand whisk to create a lump-free batter resembling thick cream. Finally, pass the batter through a sieve into another bowl or jug. Leave the batter to rest for a minimum of 30 minutes in the kitchen, longer if possible.

3. Heat the oven to 220°C.

4. Place a pea-sized piece of your chosen fat into a 4-hole Yorkshire pudding tin or 12-hole muffin tin and heat in the oven until the fat is slightly smoking.

5. Give the batter another good whisk, add 2 tablespoons of cold water, one-third fill each hole of your tin with batter, and return quickly to the oven. Cook for 20–25 minutes or until the puddings are golden and risen.

6. Serve the Yorkshire puddings immediately.

Kitchen notes: If you have any leftover batter, repeat step 5 without adding any water until all the batter is used up.

Onion Gravy Filled Yorkshire Pudding

The onion gravy is the simplest, quickest, and most delicious filling for Yorkshire puddings. Add a few chunks of leftover roast meat and vegetables from Sunday lunch for a more substantial dish. Onion gravy is also perfect for serving with toad in the hole.

Use a traditional 4-hole Yorkshire pudding tin to make individual puddings.

serves 4

1 quantity of Yorkshire pudding batter (page 14)
2 tablespoons beef dripping/lard/vegetable oil
gravy:
2 tablespoons oil
2 tablespoons butter
2 medium red onions, peeled and thinly sliced
½ teaspoon sugar
1 teaspoon balsamic vinegar
750 ml beef stock
4 teaspoons cornflour
4 teaspoons cold water
salt and black pepper

1. Make the Yorkshire pudding batter and leave it to rest for a minimum of 30 minutes to several hours.

2. Meanwhile, make the onion gravy: over a gentle heat, melt the oil and butter in a large saucepan. Add the onions and cover with a lid. Cook slowly for 10 minutes or until the onions are soft and translucent.

3. Add the sugar and balsamic vinegar and stir well. Cover and cook for 5 minutes. Add the stock and boil gently uncovered for 5 minutes.

4. In a heatproof jug or bowl, mix the cornflour with the cold water a little at a time to a thin paste. Pour a little hot gravy into the starch mixture and mix thoroughly then pour into the gravy. Raise the heat to high and boil for 10 minutes until slightly thickened. Season with salt and pepper to taste. Keep warm until ready to serve.

5. Heat the oven to 220°C.

6. Put a quarter of the fat or oil into each hole of the tin and heat in the oven until slightly smoking.

7. Give the batter another good whisk, add 2 tablespoons of cold water, one-third fill each hole with batter, and return quickly to the oven. Cook for 20–25 minutes or until the puddings are golden and risen

8. Serve the Yorkshire puddings immediately smothered with thick, glossy onion gravy – lovely.

Toad in the Hole

Toad in the hole is a massive favourite with us for a perfect midweek supper, and occasionally we even replace our Sunday roast with one.

The delightful name of the dish is believed to come from the 19th century when cooks used large dollops of seasoned, minced pork – rather than pork or flavoured sausages we are more familiar with – which when surrounded by the batter looked remarkably like toads

Make your toad in the hole in a large square roasting tin and slice into hearty slabs and serve with onion gravy – you can find the recipe on page 17.

serves 4

4 eggs, lightly beaten
235 ml whole milk
pinch of salt
125 g plain flour
3 tablespoons lard, beef dripping, or vegetable oil
6 good quality pork or flavoured sausages

1. Pour the eggs and milk into a large mixing bowl, add the salt and whisk thoroughly with an electric or hand whisk until foamy. Leave to stand for about 10 minutes.

2. Sieve the flour into the egg mixture and beat again to create a lump-free batter resembling thick cream. Finally, pass the batter through a sieve into a jug. Leave the batter to rest for a minimum of 30 minutes in the kitchen, longer if possible.

3. Heat the oven to 220°C.

4. Heat 1 tablespoon of fat or oil in a frying pan, add the sausages to the pan and cook for 10 minutes, occasionally turning until browned all over. Remove from the heat and keep to one side.

5. Put the remaining fat into a 30 x 25 cm deep roasting tin and put it into the centre of the oven. Heat until lightly smoking.

6. Remove the tin from the oven and add the sausages, spacing evenly, and return to the oven and cook for 5 minutes.

7. Carefully pour the Yorkshire pudding batter into the tin and leave to cook for 20–30 minutes or until the pudding is golden and risen.

8. Serve the toad in the hole with a generous serving of onion gravy (see page 17).

Mum's Stew and Dumplings

I love winter cooking, especially long, slow-cooked, hearty stews. Beef shin is an excellent cut of meat for this type of cooking. Add suet dumplings and you have the ultimate comfort food.

Thanks to my lovely mum who often made this for us, and I have very fond memories of her when I cook it.

serves 6

4 tablespoons vegetable oil
500 g shin of beef, off the bone, cut into thick pieces
4 tablespoons plain flour
150 ml port or red wine
1 medium yellow onion, peeled and thickly sliced
4 garlic cloves, peeled
1 carrot, peeled and thickly sliced
1 large leek, cleaned and cut into thick rings
2 celery sticks, thickly chopped
2 tablespoons tomato puree
1 litre beef stock
1 bay leaf
tiny sprig fresh rosemary
small handful flat-leaf parsley
1 tablespoon Worcestershire sauce
salt and pepper
2 large potatoes, peeled and cut into large chunks

for the dumplings:
100 g self-raising flour
50 g chopped suet
pinch salt
cold water to mix
2 tablespoons fresh parsley, chopped

1. Preheat the oven to 150°C.

2. On the hob, heat the oil to hot in a large ovenproof casserole. In small batches, add pieces of beef and turn in the hot oil to seal. Place each batch onto a large plate and sprinkle liberally with flour.

3. Increase the heat to high, add the port or red wine, reduce by about one-third, stir well and scrape up any meat juices stuck on the bottom of the dish. Continue to cook rapidly to reduce the wine by a third.

4. Add the vegetables – except the potatoes – and tomato puree, stir well and cook for 5 minutes until soft but not browned.

5. Add the beef back to the casserole, stir and slowly add the beef stock, stirring continuously. Finally, add the bay leaf, rosemary, parsley and Worcestershire sauce.

6. Lower the heat, bring the stew to a gentle boil, then cover with a tight-fitting lid and pop it into the oven.

7. Cook for around 3 hours or until the meat is tender and beginning to fall apart. Check occasionally to make sure the casserole is not drying up; add a little boiling water if needed.

8. Meanwhile, make the dumplings.

9. Place the flour, suet and salt into a mixing bowl. Add the cold water a few tablespoons at a time, stirring to make a firm, sticky dough. Divide into 8 and roll each into a round dumpling.

10. Thirty minutes before the end of cooking time, taste the stew, season to taste, then add the chopped potatoes.

11. Finally, pop the dumplings on top of the stew and push gently into the gravy, cover with the lid, and cook for 30 minutes. Test the potatoes are cooked by piercing with the tip of a sharp knife.

12. Serve the stew in hot bowls and garnish with chopped parsley. I like Brussels sprouts or cabbage as a side dish, but you choose your favourites.

Yorkshire Game Pie

Nothing beats a hearty game pie to make a showstopping centrepiece on your table, and Boxing Day is not the same without one. Creating one takes a little effort but is not as difficult as it may seem.

Various Yorkshire game is in season from August to early in the new year and there's plenty of it given the wealth of moorland, beautiful woods, forests and fields in the county. Buy your game from either a good butcher or online, though out of season, the meat will be frozen. In this recipe I have used pheasant, wild rabbit, and venison.

serves 8

pie filling:
750 g mixed game
250 g belly pork, minced
1 teaspoon mace
1 teaspoon ground ginger
tiny pinch ground cloves
75 ml red wine
2 tablespoon brandy
sea salt flakes and freshly ground black pepper

hot water pastry:
80 g lard plus 1 extra tablespoon for greasing
80 g butter
200 ml water
pinch of sea salt
465 g plain flour plus extra for rolling

to assemble the pie:
2 tablespoon redcurrant jelly
1 tablespoon dried cranberries
1 egg yolk
2 tablespoons milk

1. Put all the pie filling ingredients into a large baking bowl, season generously with salt and pepper, stir and leave to marinate for at least an hour, up to overnight if you have time.

2. Place a colander or sieve over a large bowl and tip the marinated meat in and leave to drain while you make the pastry.

3. Lightly smear the inside of a 24 cm non-stick raised game pie mould or loose-bottomed cake tin with the extra lard and put it to one side.

4. Melt the lard, butter with the water, and salt in a saucepan over medium

heat. Put the flour into a large mixing bowl, make a well in the centre and tip the melted fat in and beat together quickly with a wooden spoon to bring the pastry together.

5. Once the pastry is cool enough to handle, tip it onto the worktop and knead for a few minutes to create a smooth, slightly sticky dough. Cut away a good third of the pastry, wrap this in a warm tea towel and put it to one side.

6. Roll the remaining pastry and carefully lay it into the mould. Next, tear off a small piece of excess pastry, roll it into a ball and using this ball press the pastry into the decorative crevices and corners of the tin; this pastry is very forgiving and should it tear, it will pinch together very easily. Finally, check there are no holes; plug it with a bit of pastry if you find one.

7. Heat the oven to 200°C.

8. Stir the redcurrant jelly and cranberries through the drained meat, then pack firmly into the mould.

9. Roll out the remaining pastry to make a lid for your pie, lay it over the meat, trim the edges, then crimp the edges firmly together.

10. Beat the egg and milk together, then generously paint a wash over the surface of the pie. Next, gather all the pastry trimmings and cut them into whatever shapes take your fancy to decorate the pie. Finally, cut two small holes into the centre of the lid of the pie to help release steam while cooking.

11. Put the pie on the middle shelf of the oven and bake for 20 minutes, then lower the heat to 160°C and cook for a further 2 hours. Some juices may run from the steam holes, but these add a delicious caramelly character to the pastry, so do not worry. The pie is cooked when the pastry has slightly shrunk away from the mould.

12. Remove from the oven, place on a cooling rack and leave for several hours or overnight to cool completely.

13. Serve cold, preferably never straight from the fridge; room temperature is best, or warm with mashed potatoes and red cabbage.

14. The pie will keep well in the refrigerator for a week wrapped in greaseproof paper.

Steak and Yorkshire Terrier Ale Pie

Steak and ale is a proper Yorkshire pie full of great ingredients and lovely memories – and my mum's pie was legendary. This pie was permanently on the menu at my restaurant, which bears testament to its solid Yorkshire heritage. Do not be alarmed using Yorkshire Terrier in the pie; it is not meat but a lovely ale from York Brewery.

serves 4

1 quantity of shortcrust pastry (page 185)

the filling:

25 g plain flour

sea salt and freshly ground black pepper

25 g salted butter

1 tablespoon vegetable oil

900 g thick braising steak, cut into 2.5 cm chunks

2 large onions, peeled and thinly sliced

2 carrots, peeled and roughly chopped

2 teaspoons Worcestershire sauce

2 teaspoons tomato puree

500 ml Yorkshire Terrier ale (or your favourite)

500 ml beef stock

1 large egg, beaten

1. Put the flour into a shallow dish large enough to hold all the meat, season with a generous pinch of salt and pepper.

2. Heat the butter and oil in a large ovenproof casserole dish, to hot. Add the steak in three separate batches. Brown all over, then put into the dish of flour, rolling it around to coat all the pieces.

3. Add the onions and carrots to the pan you seared the meat in and cook gently for 2 minutes. Add the beef back to the pan, add the Worcestershire sauce, tomato puree, beer and stock. Season with black pepper and salt, stir and bring to a boil.

4. Cover the casserole, reduce to a gentle simmer and cook slowly for 2 hours until the meat is tender and the sauce is thickened.

5. Meanwhile, make the pastry and rest it while the stew is cooking.

6. Take the casserole from the heat, lift the casserole lid, stir, then re-cover leaving a small gap to allow steam to escape and cool completely.

7. When you are ready to cook the pie, heat the oven to 200°C.

8. Roll the pastry to 1 cm thick and large enough to line the bottom and sides of an oblong 24 cm x 5 cm pie dish and cut a lid for your pie dish. Line the dish and trim to size.

9. Using a slotted spoon, lift the meat and vegetables from the casserole, allowing the gravy to drain back in, put the meat into the pie, fill until the filling is ever so slightly higher than the rim.

10. Sit a pie funnel in the centre of the pie to support the pastry lid and stop it from sinking into the filling. Lay the lid over, trim to fit, and crimp the edges using your thumb and first finger to create a good, tight seal.

11. Brush with beaten egg and make a tiny hole in the centre to reveal the pie funnel. Bake in the centre of the oven for 30–35 minutes until the pastry is crisp and golden.

12. Serve piping hot with the leftover reheated gravy from the casserole dish, roast or mashed potatoes and fresh vegetables.

Extra Creamy Egg Custard

These delightful treats have been around for centuries and can be found all over Britain, but here in Yorkshire, we do have a bit of a passion for them. Most bakeries sell them, but nothing beats making your own. I love to eat them at their best while still slightly wobbly and warm.

I was taught at school to make this in a large deep tin, but you can make individual ones if you wish. Use a fluted tin for a more traditional look, though it will not spoil the taste if you don't have one.

serves 6

1 quantity sweet pastry (page 186)
for the filling:
350 ml double cream
350 ml whole milk
1 vanilla pod, split but not scraped
3 whole free-range eggs + 3 egg yolks
40 g caster sugar
1 fresh nutmeg

1. Make the pastry and rest it wrapped in clingfilm while you make the filling.

2. Bring the cream, milk and vanilla pod to a boil in a pan.

3. Whisk the eggs, egg yolks and sugar together in a large baking bowl using a hand or electric whisk. Then, constantly whisking, slowly pour the boiled milk and cream onto the egg mixture.

4. Strain the custard through a fine sieve into a jug or bowl. Put the vanilla pod back into the custard and chill in the fridge while making the pastry case.

5. Heat the oven to 200°C.

6. Lightly grease a 25 cm deep, fluted tart tin, line with pastry and bake blind (page 187).

7. Once baked, lower the oven temperature to 130°C.

8. Gently pour the custard mix into the baked pastry case and generously grate fresh nutmeg all over the surface. Bake for 10 minutes, turn the oven down to 100°C and continue to cook until the tart has set. Check after the first hour and then regularly until fully set.

9. Once cooked, remove the tart from the oven and leave to settle for an hour on a cooling rack, then refrigerate, lightly covered with baking paper until needed. Bring the custard tart back to room temperature before serving.

Super Sweet Yorkshire Treacle Tart

Treacle tart is a true Yorkshire favourite, but a tart not for the faint-hearted as it is very sweet thanks to a generous amount of golden syrup and black treacle. The sweetness though is slightly offset by the lemon zest and juice which also gives it a lovely citrusy tang.

The tart makes a lovely dessert served warm and with ice cream.

serves 6–8

350 g shortcrust pastry (page 185)
1 tablespoon butter
300 g golden syrup
1 tablespoon black treacle
1 lemon, zest and juice
4 eggs
3 tablespoons fresh breadcrumbs

1. Make the pastry.

2. Lightly grease a 22 cm loose-bottomed tart tin with butter. Roll out the pastry to 5 mm thick and large enough to line the base and sides of the tin. Rest the tart in the fridge for 15–30 minutes.

3. Heat the oven to 180°C. Put a baking sheet into the centre of the oven while it is heating up.

4. Mix the golden syrup, treacle, lemon zest and juice in a large mixing bowl. Next, beat the eggs in another bowl or jug and add to the treacle mixture. Finally, stir in the breadcrumbs.

5. Put the pastry case onto the baking sheet in the oven and carefully pour in the egg and treacle mixture.

6. Bake for 20–25 minutes, until both the crust and filling are golden brown and slightly firm to the touch. Once cooked, remove it from the oven and pop it onto a cooling rack in its tin for 10 minutes.

7. If serving warm as a pudding, serve at once with crème fraiche or vanilla ice cream, otherwise leave it to go cold and store in an airtight tin where it will keep well for a few days.

Traditional Yorkshire Parkin

Sticky, moist, and ever so comforting, a traditional Yorkshire parkin is the stuff of winter nights and for me has special memories of eating it on Bonfire Night. Parkin truly is one of the best cakes for enjoying a taste of Yorkshire.

The cake is straightforward to make but needs a little planning ahead as it is best kept before eating to allow the flavours to develop and for the cake to become sticky and moist.

Parkin is also a very versatile cake and can be a pudding and even a topping for other dishes. My favourite always will be with a cup of tea, but look at the other suggestions below for inspiration.

serves 6–8

170 g soft butter, plus a little extra for greasing
110 g soft, dark brown sugar
120 g black treacle
80 g golden syrup
125 g medium oatmeal
200 g self-raising flour
1 teaspoon baking powder
3 teaspoons ground ginger
2 teaspoons mace (or nutmeg if you don't have any)
1 teaspoon mixed spice
1 egg
2 tablespoons milk

1. Heat the oven to 140°C, grease a 22 x 12 cm (2 lb) loaf tin with butter.

2. Melt the butter, sugar, treacle, and golden syrup in a large saucepan over gentle heat. Avoid boiling the mixture; it simply needs to melt together.

3. Place all the dry ingredients and spices into a roomy baking bowl and stir. Gradually add the melted butter/treacle mixture and stir well, coating all the dry ingredients.

4. Beat the eggs with the milk, stir into the cake batter, pour the mixture into the prepared tin, and cook for 1½ hours until set and a dark, golden brown.

5. Remove the parkin from the oven, place the tin on a cooling rack and leave it to cool in the tin. Once cooled, remove from the tin and store in an airtight container for a minimum of 3–5 days (if you can resist eating it) to allow the flavours to develop and the cake to become sticky and moist.

Five uses for Yorkshire parkin, though I am sure there are many more:

- Replace the cake in a traditional trifle with slices of parkin for a lovely ginger flavour. Sprinkle the cake with a bit of syrup from stem ginger and use fine slivers of the ginger as decoration.

- Move over sticky toffee pudding, serve warm parkin drenched with hot toffee sauce, custard or vanilla ice cream.

- Serve warm Yorkshire parkin with stewed or roasted Yorkshire rhubarb and a little thick cream.

- Should you ever have any leftover parkin, leave the cake to dry a little and break into crumbs to use as a topping for ice cream, or if you are making ice cream, add the crumbs before churning.

- Stir the crumbs into a cheesecake mixture.

Roasted Rhubarb and Vanilla Crumble

Who doesn't love a rhubarb crumble? Growing up, ours was made with Dad's rhubarb from the allotment; now, I love it with famous Yorkshire forced rhubarb in early spring.

Forcing rhubarb crowns began purely by accident in the physic garden at Chelsea in 1817 when rhubarb crowns accidentally were covered with soil which revealed a way of growing rhubarb that resulted in a sweeter, tender and less astringent stalk.

There are three things needed for the successful forcing of rhubarb: it needs the cold, lots of water and a good supply of nitrogen, all of which it turned out West Yorkshire has in abundance and is how what is now known as the "Rhubarb Triangle" here in Yorkshire came about. The triangle sits in a frost pocket; the nearby Pennine hills supply ample rainwater, and nitrogen came originally courtesy of the shoddy (waste wool) from the nearby woollen mills and was used as fertiliser. Back then, a good rail network also helped in distributing the rhubarb quickly and easily to the rest of the UK and beyond.

The huge sheds used for forcing are entirely dark save for candlelight which, contrary to belief, is not for the rhubarb to grow but for the pickers to be able to see what they are doing. Once in the sheds, the plant is deprived of light and food and 'forces' the root to begin growing the rhubarb stalks. It grows so quickly that you can hear the 'popping' sound as the stalks are pushed out from the bud if it is quiet in the shed.

The rhubarb would usually be stewed, but in this recipe, using forced, I roast the vegetable (yes, it is a vegetable, not a fruit) in the oven with a bit of orange juice and vanilla. Roasting helps the rhubarb keep its beautiful colour and intensifies the flavour, creating a delicious and memorable pudding. Serve with plenty of custard or vanilla ice cream.

serves 6

for the crumble:
115 g cold butter
170 g plain flour
4 tablespoons soft brown sugar
for the filling:
450 g rhubarb
2 tablespoons soft brown sugar
½ teaspoon vanilla extract
3 tablespoons orange juice

1. Place all the crumble ingredients into a large baking bowl and roughly mash together to form lumpy crumbs. Don't make the mixture too fine, aim for a rustic topping. Put the crumble into a freezer bag or box and pop it into the freezer while you roast the rhubarb.

2. Preheat the oven to 175°C.

3. Cut the rhubarb into 3 cm pieces and put into an ovenproof dish. Sprinkle over the sugar. Mix the vanilla extract with the orange juice and pour over the rhubarb, loosely cover with tin foil. Bake in the preheated oven for approximately 15 minutes or until the rhubarb is cooked through but not falling apart. Remove from the oven and leave to cool.

4. Put the rhubarb into an ovenproof dish, about 20 x 12 x 5 cm. Take the crumble from the freezer and break it up a little. Sprinkle over the rhubarb. Cook for 30–35 minutes in the centre of the oven until golden brown and bubbling. Serve at once, traditionally with custard, but vanilla ice cream is also excellent.

Wensleydale Cheese Scones

Of course, you can use any mature Cheddar for these scones, but here in Yorkshire, you can't go far wrong with some fabulous Wensleydale cheese from the famous creamery in the Dales at Hawes. I love to use their extra mature Cheddar for these scones as it gives great colour and pronounced cheese flavour and cooks well without burning.

225 g self-raising flour
1 teaspoon baking powder
½ teaspoon salt
55 g cold butter, cubed
110 g Wensleydale cheese, grated
50 ml milk
1 free-range egg

makes 6

1.   Heat the oven to 200°C.

2.   Sift the flour, baking powder and salt into a food processor. Add the butter and pulse briefly until the mixture resembles sand. Or, by hand, place the ingredients into a large baking bowl and rub it in with your fingertips.

3.   Whichever method you use, add all but a tablespoon of the cheese, and mix carefully using a dinner knife.

4.   Beat the milk with the egg and pour into the baking bowl, and again, using a dinner knife, mix everything quickly; take care not to over mix as this can make the scones dry.

5.   Using your hands, carefully bring the mixture together, pressing it firmly into a ball. Lightly flour a work surface and gently press the dough using the heel of your hand into an even 2.5 cm thickness.

6.   Using a straight edge pastry cutter, press out 4 scones taking care not to twist the cutter as this causes the scones to fall over when rising.

7.   Carefully press the remnants together and repeat the pressing and cutting of 2 more scones.

8.   Sprinkle the scones with the remaining cheese. Place onto a hot baking sheet and bake in the centre of the oven for 12–14 minutes, risen, a lovely golden colour and as light as a feather.

9.   Remove from the oven onto a cooling rack. The scones are best eaten the same day but will still be good the next if you store them in an airtight box. Serve with loads of butter and a little chutney if you like.

Individual Yorkshire Curd Tarts

Yorkshire curd tart is a true legacy recipe of the county and was created to use up leftover fresh curd from the cheese-making process.

Fresh curds can be bought from a dairy, and if you are lucky to find them, then that's wonderful but they are quite hard to come by. However, making your own is easy, but you will need to start the day before you make the tart.

serves 4

for the curds:
1 litre full cream milk
2 tablespoons rennet

for the tart:
1 quantity of pastry (page 185)
100 g unsalted butter, softened
50 g caster sugar
2 medium eggs, well beaten
pinch of salt
¼ teaspoon freshly grated nutmeg
¼ teaspoon ground allspice
1 rounded tablespoon fresh white breadcrumbs
50 g plump, seedless raisins
50 g currants

making curds:

1. Place the milk into a saucepan and over a gentle heat. Bring to 37°C using a thermometer. Remove from the heat, stir in the rennet and leave in a cool place to set. Once cooled and set, gently break up the mixture into large chunks using a fork.

2. Line a large sieve or colander with fine muslin or cheesecloth and place over a large bowl. Spoon the chunks of curd into the sieve or colander and leave to drain for at least 6 hours, preferably overnight.

the tart:

3. Roll out the pastry to 5 mm thick. Grease and line 4, 4 x 10 cm tart tins with the pastry. Prick the bases all over with a fork. Chill in the refrigerator for 15 minutes then bake blind (page 187).

4. Cream the butter and sugar together in a large baking bowl until fluffy and light, and pale in colour. Tip the curd mixture into the creamed butter.

5. Add the beaten eggs, salt, nutmeg, allspice and beat well until all the ingredients are well incorporated. Finally, stir in the breadcrumbs, raisins and currants.

6. Pour the curd mixture into the prepared tart cases and bake in the oven for 20 minutes until golden brown. Leave them to cool, then serve. The curd tarts are best eaten slightly warm and at best within 24 hours of making them.

STARTERS,
SOUPS AND
SMALL PLATES

Coconut Shrimp

Biting into this delicious coconut-coated shrimp is scrumptious. Eat them on their own or with a sweet-spicy sauce or mango dip.

serves 4

12 large unshelled, tail-on shrimp, fresh or frozen (cooked/uncooked)
65 g plain flour
1 teaspoon baking powder
¼ teaspoon salt
1 egg
70 ml cold sparkling water
65 g shredded coconut
120 ml coconut oil, or another plain oil vegetable

1.   If your shrimp is frozen, defrost slowly and thoroughly before cooking.

2.   Make the batter by mixing the dry ingredients in a bowl. Break the egg into the mixture, add the water, and whisk to create a smooth batter.

3.   Spread coconut over a plate and place this next to the batter. Holding the shrimp by the tail, dip it into the batter, then at once into the coconut. Roll it around, making sure it is completely coated. Lay the batter-covered shrimp on kitchen paper. Continue until all the shrimp are coated.

4.   Heat the oil in a deep frying pan over a medium-high heat. Slide the shrimp a few at a time into the hot oil, lower the heat to medium and fry quickly for about 20 seconds on each side.

6.   Remove the shrimp from the oil once they are a medium golden brown. Drain on kitchen paper. Serve hot straight from the pan.

Smoked Haddock Tartare Terrine

In the early days of my cookery school in France and Sweden, this was an excellent dish to teach those all-important knife skills that make cooking so much easier and quicker once mastered. The fish, vegetables and even the parsley need to be chopped meticulously so they are all the same size and the finished terrine looks as good as it tastes. It was always a fun exercise as any not diced well were ceremoniously rejected and thrown into the stockpot – not the fish though, that went to the cat.

serves 4

120 g cucumber, peeled, seeded, finely diced
2 teaspoons sea salt flakes plus extra for seasoning
60 g potato, peeled and finely diced
20 g smoked haddock, cut into 5 mm dice
30 g sweet red pepper, deseeded and finely diced
2 shallots, finely diced
3 teaspoons chopped parsley
3 tablespoons mayonnaise (shop-bought is fine)
4 generous tablespoons sour cream
garnish:
1 small avocado
2 fresh tomatoes
fresh herbs of choice

1. Sprinkle the cucumber with 1 teaspoon of salt and leave to drain for 10 minutes.

2. Boil the potatoes in lightly salted water for 3 minutes maximum. Drain, then lay on kitchen paper to dry.

3. Rinse the cucumber under running cold water, then pat dry with kitchen paper.

4. In a bowl, mix the fish and all the diced vegetables, the chopped parsley and mayonnaise.

5. Place a 7 cm pastry ring in the centre of a serving plate and spoon the vegetable and fish mixture into it; press very firmly.

6. Next, smooth the surface with the back of a spoon. Press a slight indentation in the centre of the mixture and top with a dollop of sour cream. Then finally, loosen the ring and lift it away, taking care not to disturb the terrine.

7. Cover with clingfilm if necessary and refrigerate until ready to serve.

8. When ready to serve, garnish with chopped avocado and tomato and fresh herbs as you wish.

Thai-inspired Salmon and Sweet Potato Fishcakes

These fishcakes are seriously quick and easy to make with lots of room to play with the ingredients using different spices, herbs or fish. Make them for lunch with a quick salad or dress them up with loads of fresh seasonal vegetables for dinner.

serves 4

450 g sweet potato, peeled
150 g salmon fillets, skinned
3 teaspoons Thai green curry paste
3 tablespoons panko breadcrumbs
1 tablespoon fresh coriander leaf, chopped
salt and pepper
3 tablespoons vegetable oil for frying

1.   Cut the sweet potato roughly into 2.5 cm chunks. Place into a pan of cold water with a pinch of salt, bring to the boil and cook until soft, about 10 minutes. Once cooked, drain and put back into the pan over a medium heat for 5 minutes to help dry them.

2.   While the potatoes are cooking, steam the salmon fillets over boiling water for 7 minutes. Once cooked put to one side to cool.

3.   Put the curry paste in a bowl, add the sweet potato and mash with a fork or masher.

4.   Flake the cooled salmon, add to the sweet potato mash and gently stir to combine.

5.   Add 1 tablespoon of panko, the coriander and a little salt and pepper to the fishcake mixture and carefully stir without breaking the fish up too much.

6.   Divide the mix into 4 and roll each into a ball, then carefully flatten to create a thick fishcake.

7.   Place the remaining panko in a shallow dish and gently press the fishcakes into it, one at a time, turning the fishcake until covered all over with the breadcrumbs. Pop the fishcakes into the fridge for 30 minutes to chill.

8.   Heat the oil in a frying pan until hot but not smoking. Cook the fishcakes for 3–4 minutes on each side or until a crisp golden brown; they are soft and may break a little, but no worries, they still taste amazing. Keep warm in the oven until ready to serve.

Crab Roll with Avocado Mayonnaise and Summer Pickles

This recipe is a deliciously easy way to serve crab that oozes summer and the seaside. Make the pickles ahead of time and make plenty to use as a condiment on other dishes.

If you are feeling extravagant, or have some leftovers, try switching out the crab meat for lobster. You won't be disappointed.

serves 4

for the pickle:
120 ml apple cider
   vinegar
100 g caster sugar
½ teaspoon sea salt
1 carrot, thickly grated
½ red onion, thinly
   sliced
10 g radishes, thinly
   sliced

for the mayonnaise:
1 large ripe avocado
120 g mayonnaise
1 tablespoon natural
   yoghurt
finely grated zest and
   juice of 1 lime
few drops of Tabasco
   sauce

for the roll:
4 brioche rolls, split into
   2 lengthwise
300 g white crab meat
3 tablespoons fresh
   chives, snipped
1 pinch red chilli flakes
crisp salad leaves

1. Pour the vinegar into a saucepan, add the sugar and bring to a simmer and stir until the sugar dissolves, add the salt and leave to cool.

2. Put the carrot, onion and radish into a glass or stainless-steel bowl, pour the cooled vinegar over, cover and leave to marinate for 4–6 hours.

3. Next, make your mayonnaise when the pickles are ready. Cut the avocado in half, remove the stone and scoop out the flesh with a spoon and put into a food processor – or you can use a hand blender – with the mayonnaise, yoghurt, lime and Tabasco and blend until creamy.

4. Lightly toast the brioche and put on 4 serving plates. Stir the crab, chives and chilli through the avocado mayonnaise. Lay a couple of salad leaves on each roll, then pile the crab filling on top and dress with a bit of pickle. Serve immediately.

A Magnificent Coastline and Beautiful Rivers

I do not find it hard to boast about the coast and rivers in Yorkshire. We are so blessed to have both, which, apart from being beautiful places to go – Runswick Bay is a personal favourite – supply the county and export a vast array of fish and seafood around the world. There is now even a company producing Yorkshire caviar.

Sadly, though still fantastic, the industry is a fraction of what it once was as a keystone of local employment along the coast with the decline of classic trawl fleets. In the 1990s, there were 27 boats out catching cod and haddock out of Whitby; now (2022), there's only one.

However, according to the Yorkshire Wildlife Trust, which supports, funds and manages projects in partnership with the local fishing industry to minimise the impact on the marine environment, an emergent and buoyant shellfish fishery has continued to develop within Yorkshire's waters.

Yorkshire is Europe's lobster capital, with Bridlington the largest lobster port followed by Scarborough, and though Whitby lobster is better known, it is only third. The county is famed for its crab; few haven't heard or tasted the famous Fortune's Kippers. There's mackerel, Scarborough sole, Bridlington bass, squid, whiting, pollack, sea trout and more. And then there's the freshwater fish with salmon, brown and rainbow trout and more.

The best place to find out more about what fish is available and when, wherever you are, not just in Yorkshire, is to make friends with your fishmonger. They can advise on what is available, will prepare the fish for you and advise how to cook it. There are great fishmongers in the county; you can see a few of them on page 196 along with some fabulous smokehouses, both those well-known and some excellent newcomers who are helping to make even more of the fish and seafood available here in Yorkshire.

Pan-Fried Mackerel with Yorkshire Rhubarb

As if Yorkshire rhubarb isn't the best thing ever in a pie or crumble, it is also the perfect partner to oily fish and works very well with fresh mackerel as the slight tartness in the rhubarb cuts through any oiliness.

If you can't get Yorkshire forced rhubarb, use regular. It may not look as pretty on the plate, but it will still taste as good.

serves 2

4–5 stalks Yorkshire rhubarb
2–3 tablespoons cold water
1 tablespoon light brown sugar
4 tablespoons plain flour
sea salt and freshly ground black
    pepper

2 fresh mackerel fillets
2 tablespoons extra virgin olive oil
2 tiny sprigs of fresh rosemary
1 tablespoon capers, drained

1. Preheat the oven to 200°C. Wipe the rhubarb stalks with a damp cloth, then cut into 5 cm lengths. Place into a roasting tin and sprinkle with 2–3 tablespoons of cold water followed by the sugar.

2. Cover the tin with a sheet of foil and pop the tin into the preheated oven. Cook the rhubarb for 15 minutes or until it has softened but is still holding its shape. Leave the rhubarb to cool, then drain through a sieve and reserve the juices given off.

3. Season the flour with a little salt and pepper. Dip the mackerel fillets into the flour, skin side down. Tap the fillet gently to remove any excess flour. Heat the oil in a large frying pan, and place the fillets in the oil, again skin side down. Sprinkle with the rosemary.

4. Add the cooked rhubarb to the pan, followed by the capers. Stir gently, then remove both the rhubarb and the fish and keep warm. Finally, add the reserved rhubarb juices to the frying pan, stir well and cook for one minute.

5. Serve the fish on hot plates with the rhubarb, capers and with the juices poured over.

Summer Tomato Consommé

Tomato consommé is not a clear tomato soup; it is a clear broth bursting with tomato and basil flavour, which also happens to be clear.

The consommé can be made using only fresh tomatoes, but unless you have sweet summer tomatoes straight from the vine, use the rich tomato sauce on page 183 as the foundation for your consommé as it will bring a punchy tomato taste and extra sweetness by adding in a few fresh tomatoes.

Once you have the sauce, then clarify as I was taught at the Escoffier school in Paris; it may sound complicated, but it is not. The gently cooked egg whites coagulate and create a superfine 'sieve' to clear the soup while retaining all the flavour. The result is all the tastes of summer in a clear liquid.

serves 6

1 litre of water
1 quantity of tomato sauce (page 183)
250 g fresh ripe tomatoes, chopped
    and deseeded
6 large basil leaves
3 egg whites

1 teaspoon sugar
garnish:
2 fresh tomatoes, deseeded and
    diced
Basil or chervil leaves to garnish
    (optional)

1. Pour the water into a stockpot or large pan, stir in the tomato sauce and put it to one side.

2. Blitz the fresh tomatoes with the basil leaves in a food processor. Add the egg whites and sugar and blitz again until all the ingredients are well mixed. Pour this mixture into the stockpot with the sauce and water and stir.

3. Put the stockpot onto medium heat and bring to a gentle boil whisking all the time. Simmer gently for 15 minutes until the egg whites start to set and form a crust on the surface.

4. Line a fine sieve with a piece of clean muslin or a tea towel that has been washed in plain water (see note below). Over a large bowl, gently ladle the egg white crust into the sieve. Then slowly, a ladle at a time, pour the consommé from the stockpot over the crust, allowing time to pass through the crust and sieve before adding any more. Do not force it, or the consommé will become cloudy.

5. Return the clear consommé to the pan and reheat to hot, not boiling, intensifying the flavour.

6. Cool the soup, cover and refrigerate until required if not serving immediately.

7. Reheat the soup to hot but not boiling and divide between six hot soup plates; garnish with diced tomatoes, basil or chervil if using and serve immediately.

Kitchen notes: a muslin or tea towel washed in detergent can pass that taste to the consommé, so make sure it has no scent before using.

Creamy Butternut Squash and Apple Soup

serves 6

4 tablespoons butter
2 small Granny Smith apples, peeled and diced
1 medium yellow onion, diced
500 g butternut squash, peeled and cut into 2–3 cm chunks
1 x 400 ml tin coconut milk
1 litre vegetable stock
1 teaspoon Maldon sea salt, or similar
garnish:
tiny pinch cinnamon, optional
fresh basil leaves
½ teaspoon chilli flakes

1. Gently melt the butter in a large saucepan over medium heat. Stir the apples, onion and squash through the butter, making sure all are covered. Raise the heat slightly and cook for 10 minutes until softened slightly.

2. Pour the coconut milk and stock into the vegetables, bring to a gentle boil, reduce the heat, then lower the heat and simmer for 45 minutes or until the squash and apples are tender.

3. Taste and add salt as needed. Then, blend the soup using a hand blender or in batches in a food processor to make a smooth, creamy soup.

4. Stir through the cinnamon if using and garnish the soup with basil leaves and a very light sprinkling of chilli flakes as you like.

Super Easy Pea and Mint Soup

This soup was an absolute favourite at my cookery school in Tuscany as it is a light soup that is quick and easy to make and delicious.

Yorkshire is famous for its peas grown mainly in the east and southern area of the county and if you can get some, great, but do not be put off making this incredible spring-summer soup if you can't; use any fresh or frozen peas that are available to you.

serves 4

1 tablespoon extra virgin olive oil + extra for serving
25 g butter
1 medium red onion, peeled and finely chopped
1 garlic clove, peeled and finely chopped
750 g fresh Yorkshire peas, shelled, but for ease use frozen peas
75 g mint leaves only, roughly chopped
1 litre vegetable stock, a stock cube is fine
sea salt and freshly ground pepper, to taste
75 g Parmesan, or Yorkshire pecorino cheese, freshly grated

1. Gently heat the oil and butter in a large saucepan, add the chopped onion and cook over gentle heat for 10 minutes or until the onion is soft but not brown. Stir continuously to make sure the onion does not burn. Add the garlic and cook for a further 3 minutes, again stirring.

2. Add ¾ each of the peas, mint, and the stock. Cover the saucepan with a tight-fitting lid and cook on medium heat for 10 minutes.

3. Once cooked, blend the soup in a food processor to create a thick puree. Return the puree to the pan, season with salt and pepper and add the remaining peas, mint and stock. Cook for 5 minutes to ensure the newly added peas are cooked through.

4. Place a small mound of grated cheese in the centre of a warmed soup bowl. Pour the warm soup around the cheese. Drizzle with a few drops of the extra virgin olive oil.

5. Serve immediately with warm, crusty bread on the side.

6. This soup is also delicious cold, but not chilled.

Corn Soup

Brighten up the day with a super tasty, easy sweetcorn soup that can be made any time of the year using fresh or frozen kernels. Even better, you can adjust this basic recipe, which on its own is already lovely, into many more great soups with the addition of cooked chicken (make sure it is heated right through) or, stir in chopped fresh herbs like tarragon, parsley or chervil.

serves 4

2 tablespoons unsalted butter
1 tablespoon extra virgin olive oil
1 medium onion, finely chopped
2 cloves garlic, finely chopped
500 g fresh or frozen sweetcorn
    kernels
125 g potatoes, peeled and roughly
    chopped

2 fresh bay leaves
1 litre chicken stock
1 pinch of sea salt flakes
1 pinch of freshly ground black
    pepper
½ to 1 teaspoon chilli flakes, to
    taste, optional

1. Melt the butter and the olive oil in a large saucepan. Add the onion and cook for 5 minutes on low heat, then add the garlic and gently cook for 5 more minutes. Stir from time to time.

2. Add the sweetcorn and the potato and stir. Cook for 2 minutes, then add the bay leaves and the stock. Bring to a gentle simmer and cook uncovered for 20 minutes.

3. Remove the soup from the heat and leave to cool for 2 minutes. Remove the bay leaf and blend the soup in a food processor or a hand blender until silky smooth. Return the soup to the pan and bring back to a gentle simmer, taste and add salt flakes and black pepper if needed.

4. Serve the soup in warm bowls garnished with chilli flakes and a few more twists of black pepper. Serve hot with crusty bread and butter.

Strawberry Soup Recipe

If you thought soups are only made with vegetables, then think again. In Scandinavian countries, fruit soups are hugely popular and have been part of the food culture forever. I was introduced to this delightful way of serving fruit by my lovely friend Lena in Stockholm when we worked together at the Grand Hotel's Franska Matsalen dining room, where I held cookery courses.

serves 4

450 g of fresh strawberries
½ teaspoon Szechuan or
    black pepper
1 tablespoon sugar
½ lemon, zest only
75 g mascarpone cheese
½ teaspoon vanilla extract
1 teaspoon icing sugar
2 teaspoons of good quality
    balsamic vinegar
Greek basil for decoration

1. Place the strawberries in a mixing bowl, add the pepper, sugar and zest. Stir gently, cover with a tea cloth and leave in the fridge for 1 hour.

2. Remove the strawberries from the fridge and tip them into a food processor, or you can use a hand blender, blitz until very smooth and foamy. Put to one side, cover again with a cloth and leave to settle while making the cream.

3. Whisk the mascarpone cheese with the vanilla and icing sugar until light and airy. Pop the bowl into the fridge to chill slightly along with 4 soup plates or bowls.

4. To serve, ladle the strawberry soup into the chilled plates with a scoop of the whipped mascarpone in the centre. Dot with the balsamic and decorate with tiny leaves of Greek or regular basil. Serve at once.

Cauliflower Chowder

Cauliflower is an immensely versatile vegetable which also happens to taste rather good thanks to all the vegetables, the sharp, green apples and finishing with a good dollop of Greek yoghurt.

serves 4

25 g unsalted butter
1 small carrot, peeled, roughly chopped
1 small white onion, peeled, roughly chopped
1 stick celery, roughly chopped
2 cloves garlic, peeled and finely chopped
2 tablespoons parsley, chopped
1 large cauliflower
250 g potatoes, peeled and cut into 1 cm cubes
1.25 litres vegetable or chicken stock
100 g thick Greek yoghurt
sea salt and freshly ground black pepper
Your favourite herbs or crispy, fried onions (optional)

1. Melt the butter in a large saucepan. Place the carrot, onion, celery, garlic and parsley into a food processor and pulse to chop finely or chop by hand if you don't have a processor. Add the vegetables to the butter and cook on medium heat, stirring occasionally until soft, about 10 minutes.

2. Break the cauliflower florets into tiny pieces and once the vegetables are softened, add the cauliflower and potatoes, stir, and cook for 5 minutes. Add the stock, bring to a boil, lower the heat and simmer until the cauliflower is tender but still slightly firm.

3. Use a slotted spoon to lift out half the cauliflower and place it into a bowl and put to one side; should you pick up any of the other vegetables, just pop them back into the pan.

4. Spoon the liquid and vegetables into a food processor, or use a hand blender, and pulse to create a creamy but not smooth soup; it should remain chunky. The potatoes, however, will break up and act as a thickener so don't worry about this. Return the soup to the pan, bring to a gentle simmer and cook for 15 minutes to reduce slightly.

5. Add the Greek yoghurt and stir through, finally; add the cauliflower pieces and stir again. Cook on medium heat for a further 5 minutes, checking the small pieces of cauliflower do not go mushy.

6. Taste the soup, add salt and pepper to taste and serve in warmed bowls, garnished with a few of your favourite herbs or crispy, fried onions if you have any. The soup is best eaten the day it is made, though if refrigerated will keep for another day but not longer.

Chicken Caesar Salad Wrap

serves 4

for the filling:
4 medium-sized free-range skinless chicken breasts
2 tablespoons olive oil
salt and freshly ground pepper
for the dressing:
1 small clove garlic, crushed
3 small anchovy fillets
1 free-range egg yolk
½ teaspoon Dijon mustard
2 teaspoons lemon juice
120 ml extra virgin olive oil
salt and freshly ground pepper for seasoning
or
in a hurry, use 4 tablespoons of your favourite Caesar salad dressing
to finish:
6 soft wraps
1 romaine lettuce, finely shredded
55 g Parmesan shavings

1. One at a time, slightly flatten the chicken breasts with the back of a meat cleaver, meat mallet or rolling pin. Then brush the flattened breasts with olive oil and season with a tiny pinch of salt and pepper.

3. Heat a griddle pan to hot, add the oil-covered breasts and cook for 5 minutes on each side, lightly pressing from time to time to create charred grill lines. Once cooked, keep to one side covered with a tea towel to rest.

4. Make the dressing by blending the garlic and anchovies with a hand blender or pounding in a pestle and mortar. Put the paste into a small bowl, add the yolk, mustard and lemon juice, then whisking constantly, add the olive oil a few drops at a time until thick and creamy, season to taste.

6. Reheat the griddle pan and heat the wraps on one side until lightly charred and warmed through. On the un-charred side of the wraps, spread them generously with the dressing. Then, rip the chicken into shreds and divide it into six.

8. Place a pile of chicken in the middle of each wrap, add the lettuce and Parmesan. Make a generous fold from the bottom of the wrap, then roll tightly. Serve the wraps warm or cold; they are great for lunchboxes, parties, and picnics.

Yorkshire Asparagus

As I drive around Yorkshire from late April through into June, I am constantly on the lookout for signs announcing "asparagus for sale". Its appearance is not just the promise of buying, cooking and eating this wonderful vegetable but is also, for me, synonymous with the arrival of summer.

Imported asparagus is available almost year-round, but I refuse to buy the wax paper wrapped bundles jetted in from southern continents and look as taut, rigid and lifeless as a three-day-old corpse. There are many growers in Yorkshire, and they all need our support.

When buying, look for bright, green, evenly coloured, firm and unwrinkled spears with tight buds whenever you can. You can keep it for a couple of days, and I have found the best way to store asparagus is like a bunch of flowers, in a glass of cold water in the fridge.

When asparagus is in season, I like it unadulterated, simply slathered with salted, clarified butter – delicious. Sauces are lovely, too, and there are endless lists of them, usually based on hollandaise – the sauce that has reduced many competent cooks to tears. However, if you are not too strict about using machines, hollandaise can be achieved with near perfect results in a food processor.

Cold, cooked asparagus tips are lovely in a salad, tossed into hot pasta with fresh spring vegetables and make fantastic risotto. It is also possible to buy misshapen bundles of asparagus cheaply, which I use to make soup and purees, which freeze well.

Bringing that spring goodness into a salad is another way I enjoy eating it. Here, asparagus meets Tenderstem® broccoli – an exciting alternative to broccoli – and peas, and another super vegetable grown extensively in Yorkshire. The dressing is light with avocado, citrus, and a little feta cheese for saltiness. Eat piled high on your plate with thick slices of sourdough or as a side dish.

Asparagus and Tenderstem Salad

serves 2

250 g fresh asparagus spears, woody end removed
250 g Tenderstem®, any tough ends on the stem removed
2 tablespoons extra virgin olive oil
sea salt to taste
1 ripe avocado, pit removed, and flesh scooped out
2 tablespoons sour cream
2 tablespoons lime juice
20 g coriander leaves
75 g fresh or frozen peas
50 g feta cheese, crumbled

1. Place the asparagus and broccoli into a large bowl, drizzle with olive oil and a light sprinkle of salt.

2. Heat a griddle or frying pan over medium heat. Add the asparagus and the broccoli and cook for 6 minutes, turning the vegetables often. Remove from the pan and leave to cool on kitchen paper.

3. Blitz the avocado flesh, sour cream, lime juice and coriander in a food processor or blender to create a silky dressing. Taste and add salt but be sparing as the cheese is salty.

4. Bring a small pan of water to a gentle boil, add the peas, and cook for a few minutes until just tender.

5. Pile the asparagus and broccoli onto the centre of either two salad plates or one larger plate or bowl. Sprinkle the peas and feta over and finish with a drizzle of dressing on or around the salad.

Apple and Walnut Salad

I fell in love with the combination of apples and walnuts when I lived in the Périgord region of southwest France. The area is renowned for its walnuts, appearing in many sweet and savoury dishes.

This simple salad is great served just as it is and can also be dressed up with cheeses, or to be in tune with the Périgordine style, served with leftover bits of roast duck or confit (see page 119). I will admit to also loving this salad sprinkled with tiny hot, crisp duck fat potatoes straight from the pan.

I am using a thick balsamic dressing here, but you can also lighten the salad up by simply drizzling with good walnut oil instead.

serves 4

125 g walnut halves
3 tablespoons extra virgin olive oil
2 tablespoons good quality balsamic vinegar
1 pinch sea salt flakes
1 pinch freshly ground black pepper
1 head crisp romaine lettuce, washed
2 Granny Smith apples, or similar crisp apples
1 stick celery, finely sliced
2 spring onions, finely chopped

1. Preheat the oven to 170°C.

2. Scatter the walnuts on a small baking sheet and roast for 7 minutes in the centre of the oven until a lovely golden-brown colour. Do not let them roast any longer, or they will become bitter.

3. Whisk the olive oil with a little balsamic vinegar adding a little at a time until you create a thick, glossy dressing. Taste the dressing and add a little salt and pepper as you like.

4. Chop the lettuce into chunky strips.

5. Once you are ready to serve the salad, cut the apples into quarters, remove the core and slice thickly. Then, cut the slices in half again for small chunks of apple.

6. Divide the salad strips, the celery and spring onions between bowls or into a large dish. Sprinkle the apples over, gently crush the walnuts and sprinkle onto the salad. Drizzle with the dressing and serve at once.

Alternatives:

Add a rich saltiness by topping with crumbled feta cheese, soft goat's cheese, or cubes of Roquefort cheese.

Burrata and Grilled Peaches

If you want a taste of summer, then look no further than this super-easy recipe bursting with sunshine; peaches, salad leaves, fresh herbs and tomatoes and a large fresh, ripe creamy burrata.

serves 4

2 large ripe yellow peaches or nectarines
1 large squeaky fresh burrata
10 little gem salad leaves, washed and dried
2 tablespoons mixed soft herbs – basil, parsley, chives, and mint are good
10 large cherry tomatoes, halved
1 teaspoon pine nuts
1–2 tablespoons good quality pesto
2 tablespoons extra virgin olive oil
basil leaves, for garnish

1. Heat a heavy grill pan to hot but not smoking.

2. Cut the peaches in two, prise out the stone – this should come out easily if the fruit is ripe.

3. Put the fruit, cut side down onto the hot pan and leave for 5 minutes. Resist touching or moving the fruit; you need to trust the process.

4. After 5 minutes, using a knife or small spatula, lift one of the fruit halves to see if there are grill lines; if so, pop them onto a plate and leave them to cool.

5. Carefully lift the burrata from any liquid and dry carefully with cloth or paper. Keep to one side.

6. Choose your prettiest serving dish, lay the washed little gem leaves on, then place the burrata in the centre.

7. Cut the cooled fruit halves into bite-sized pieces and scatter onto the lettuce, followed by the herbs and chopped tomatoes.

8. Heat a frying pan to hot, add the pine nuts and toast for 3 minutes. Sprinkle these over the salad.

9. Spoon the pesto over the burrata and a little over the tomatoes but use sparingly as it can easily overpower the salad.

10. Carefully open the burrata through the centre with a sharp knife to show off the creamy centre and make it easy to dip in.

11. Serve at once garnished with basil and serve with crusty bread.

If you prefer to make your pesto dressing, it is easy. See page 193.

Posh Bubble and Squeak

A plate of bubble and squeak made from the scrumptious mix of Sunday lunch leftovers and eaten on a Monday is absolutely one of my favourite meals, especially topped off with a fried egg and brown sauce. However, this 'posh' squeak recipe is for a leisurely, quick, one-pan lunch or dinner and is made from scratch for when there are no leftovers.

There are no rules for this recipe and these are my choice of vegetables and you can, of course, ring the changes any way you like. Equally, create a meat version; Yorkshire chorizo from Lishman's is a particular favourite of mine.

serves 4

450 g new potatoes, scrubbed and cut into quarters
4 tablespoons olive oil
1 tablespoon butter
225 g carrots, scrubbed and cut into large chunks
220 g savoy cabbage, finely shredded
4 tablespoons peas
4 eggs
salt and freshly ground black pepper
½ red onion, very finely sliced
115 g Yorkshire or Spanish chorizo or pancetta, cubed (optional)
small handful of flat-leaf parsley, very finely chopped

1. Bring a pan of water to a rapid boil, add the new potatoes, cook for 5 minutes only, drain and keep to one side.

2. Heat the oven to 180°C.

3. Heat a large ovenproof frying pan to medium heat, add the olive oil and butter and heat through, taking care not to burn. Add the potatoes and carrots and give them a good stir then cook in the oven for 20 minutes until the potatoes and carrots are browning on the edges.

4. Remove the pan from the oven extremely carefully, it will be very hot and I advise wrapping a tea towel around the handle and leaving it there. Add the cabbage and the peas and stir well. Then, using a spoon, make 4 wells evenly spaced around the pan and crack an egg into each well. Season the surface well with salt and pepper, then sprinkle over the onion and finally, any meat if using.

5. Place the pan back into the oven, remove the tea towel and cook for a further 10 minutes or until the egg white is set and the yolk cooked to your liking.

6. Remove from the oven, wrap the towel around the handle and leave to stand for 5 minutes. Sprinkle with chopped parsley and serve at once. I love this with a good dollop of brown sauce.

Roasted Celery Root

The humble celery root – or celeriac, as it's known – is a much-overlooked vegetable. It may not be the prettiest, but it has a fabulous flavour. Though it does taste of celery, it is much softer than the crunchy stalks, which can overwhelm other ingredients. A great way to bring out even more flavour with celeriac is to roast it, which creates a crisp exterior and soft interior.

The vegetable makes a lovely side dish for roast meats (try it with your Sunday dinner) and is a beautiful base vegetable for a soup or in a vegetable curry.

You can roast celery root in either olive oil (don't use your best extra virgin for this) or duck or goose fat – instructions for both are included in the recipe.

serves 4–6

1 large celery root, peeled and sliced roughly into 1.5 cm x 2.5 cm chunks
6 tablespoons olive oil or duck fat
sea salt
freshly ground pepper

1.   Heat the oven to 200°C.

2.   To cook with olive oil, put the celery root into a large baking bowl. Drizzle the oil over and stir well to coat all the pieces.

3.   Spread the pieces onto a heavy oven tray. Sprinkle with sea salt and freshly ground black pepper. Bake in the centre of the oven for 30 minutes until crisp and golden.

Or:

4.   For duck fat, put fat into a deep heavy-based roasting dish. Put the dish into the centre of the hot oven and heat for around 5 minutes.

5.   Put the celery root into a baking bowl, sprinkle with sea salt and a few grinds of black pepper. Stir well.

6.   Once the fat is heated, tip in the celery root, spread through the melted fat by gently shaking the pan, return to the oven and cook for 30 minutes until crisp and golden brown.

7.   You should not need to turn the celeriac during cooking if using a heavy tray or pan. However, check the cooking every 15 minutes, just in case and turn if needed. Once cooked, remove from the oven and serve at once.

School Days
and Scotch Eggs

It is funny to think that something as ordinary as a Scotch egg could have had such an impact on me, and though it didn't plot the course of the rest of my life, it certainly set me on a track.

I was 12 years old and in a cooking class at school when my teacher, Miss Kingston, taught us to make a Scotch egg. The transformation of a boiled egg, pink meat squeezed from a pack of sausages with a bit of seasoning and breadcrumbs into a fist of ridiculously delicious food astonished me. I remember smugly carrying home my precious bundle of eggs to amaze my parents with my talent and them oohing and aahing in all the right places. I was hooked on cooking from then on.

Scotch eggs were created in 1738 by Fortnum & Mason of Piccadilly, London, as convenient, easy-to-transport meals for travellers and quickly became a classic British food. But, when Britain began its love affair with all things Mediterranean and healthy, circa the eighties, the poor egg got short shrift for being unhealthy because of the deep frying in the cooking. Those who still liked one could always find them in pubs or the mass-produced ones on supermarket shelves, neither of which lived up to the glories of ones crafted by hand. I, too, forgot about them.

Thanks to chef Gordon Ramsay and others who brought this little beauty back, they now come in a slightly healthier version, half-fried and half-baked but with no loss of deliciousness. Of course, some chefs like to mess with them a little, including the likes of black pudding or wrapping delicate quails' eggs rather than hens' etc., but it is and always will be, for me, this classic sausage-wrapped recipe that is the best.

serves 6

6 fresh, free-range eggs
400 g pork sausage meat
2 tablespoons shallot, finely chopped
2 tablespoons parsley, chopped
½ teaspoon mace
1 teaspoon Worcestershire sauce
1 teaspoon sea salt
½ teaspoon freshly ground black pepper
2 tablespoons plain flour
60 g panko breadcrumbs
1 litre neutral oil for frying

1. Set a large pan of water to boil; once boiling, add 4 eggs and cook for precisely 6 minutes. Lift them one by one from the pan, tap lightly on the worktop to slightly crack the shell (this makes them easier to peel), and plunge them into a bowl of iced water to stop the eggs from cooking. Leave them there until needed.

2. Put the sausage meat, shallot, parsley, mace, Worcestershire sauce, salt, and pepper into a large bowl.

3. Now be prepared for the first messiness of making Scotch eggs – use your hands to combine all the ingredients thoroughly; then, before you wash your hands, divide the mixture into four equal-sized balls.

4. Peel the cooked eggs and dry them with kitchen paper. Then, lightly beat the remaining 2 eggs, put onto a shallow plate, the flour onto another plate, and the panko onto a third.

5. Now for the messiest part. The success of the Scotch egg is to ensure you put an even layer of sausage meat around the egg, so take a ball of sausage meat and flatten it evenly in the palm of your hand.

6. Lay the egg in the centre of the sausage meat and gently and carefully coax the sausage meat around the egg, closing your palm to ease it into place. Press with your fingers to ensure no cracks or gaps and the sausage meat is evenly spread.

7. Repeat with the remaining eggs.

8. Put the meat-covered eggs in the refrigerator for 10 minutes. Then, heat the oil in a wok on the stovetop to 180°C and preheat the oven to the same temperature.

6. Roll the meat-covered egg in the flour, then into the beaten egg, then press the egg into the panko, making sure the whole egg is covered.

7. Cook the eggs, two at a time, in the hot oil for 4–5 minutes, turning them constantly with a spoon to make sure they cook evenly to a light golden brown. Once cooked, place on a baking sheet and bake in the centre of the oven for a further 4–6 minutes.

8. Remove from the oven and eat while hot, or leave to go cold. Serve with piccalilli, pickles, or a little mustard for the perfect lunchbox, picnic, or party food.

Easy Cauliflower Cheese

Cauliflower cheese makes the most of Yorkshire cauliflowers which are not only cheap, but also nutritious and available almost year-round.

For the cheese sauce use a robust Yorkshire cheese such as extra mature Wensleydale, or Dale End Cheddar from Botton Dairy works very well. If you can't find either of these choose a mature Cheddar.

serves 6 as a side dish

1 medium cauliflower (around 450 g)
60 g butter
60 g plain flour
large pinch salt
400 ml milk
75 g grated strong cheese, plus extra for sprinkling
freshly ground black pepper

1.   Heat the oven to 200°C.

2.   Break the cauliflower into florets removing the thick central core. Steam over a pan of boiling water for 10 minutes. Remove the cauliflower from the heat and leave to cool.

3.   Place the butter, flour and a good pinch of salt into a large saucepan and stir over a low heat until you have created a thick paste.

4.   Raise the heat and add the cold milk all at once and whisk like crazy until a thick, smooth cream is formed, then cook gently for about 5 minutes. Add the grated cheese and stir again. Once the cheese has melted remove from the heat.

5.   Place the steamed florets into a baking dish large enough to hold them in one layer.

6.   Pour the cheese sauce over the cauliflower, sprinkle with a little grated cheese and a good twist of black pepper.

7.   Bake in the hot oven until the sauce is bubbling and golden brown on the top, about 30 minutes. Serve immediately. The cauliflower does heat up well the next day should you have any left over.

Mini Pumpkin Pasty Bites

I originally made these tasty mini pasties for a Harry Potter-themed party and they have since become something of a favourite, especially for parties and picnics. However, if you are making them for children, you may want to go easy with the spice.

makes 12

1 quantity of pastry (page 185)
for the filling:
375 g peeled pumpkin or squash, cut into tiny cubes
1 teaspoon medium curry powder
1 tablespoon soft brown sugar
pinch of sea salt and freshly ground black pepper
1 egg, lightly beaten

1. Preheat oven to 190°C.

2. Make the pastry, wrap in clingfilm and rest it in the fridge while you make the filling.

3. Line a baking tray with baking parchment and sprinkle on the pumpkin pieces. Next, mix the curry powder, sugar, salt and pepper and sprinkle over the pumpkin. Give the tray a little shake to make sure all the pumpkin is covered.

4. Roast for 15 minutes or until the pumpkin turns golden brown.

5. Whilst the pumpkin is cooking, roll out the pastry on a floured work surface and cut 12 x 7 cm circles, put them onto a plate and pop them in the fridge until needed.

6. Once the pumpkin is cooked, tip the cubes onto a plate, cover with a tea towel and leave to cool.

7. Gently brush the edges of the pastry circles with a little cold water and spoon a few cubes of pumpkin onto each. Fold the pastry over and pinch the edges together to seal.

8. Brush the pasties with beaten egg and put them back onto the paper-covered tray you used to cook the pumpkin.

9. Cook in the centre of the oven until the pasties are a dark golden brown, around 15 minutes.

10. Once cooked, put the pasties on a cooling rack to cool. Best eaten the same day but they will store until the next in an airtight tin.

Yorkshire Curried Lamb and Potato Pasty

We love our pasties here in Yorkshire; be they meat and veg, veg, cheese or vegan, as long as they are wrapped in buttery pastry, we will eat them.

This lamb pasty brings together Yorkshire favourites with lamb, potatoes, curry spices, peas and, of course, pastry. Make them to any size you like, small for parties, buffets and picnics, to large handheld ones for the football terraces or hungry kids.

makes 4

1 quantity shortcrust pastry (page 185)
for the filling:
150 g potatoes, Maris Piper or similar
25 g unsalted butter
50 g leeks, cleaned and finely sliced
2 teaspoons garlic, finely chopped
225 g lamb mince
1½ tablespoon medium curry powder
1 bird's eye chilli, finely chopped
1 tablespoon coriander leaves, chopped
50 g frozen peas
sea salt and freshly ground black pepper
1 egg, beaten

1. Make the pastry and roll out to the thickness of a pound coin. Then cut into 4 x 16 cm circles. Put the circles onto a plate, cover with clingfilm and rest in the fridge while you make the filling.

2. Peel and cut the potatoes roughly into 1 cm cubes. Rinse under cold water to rinse off excess starch and pat dry with kitchen paper.

3. Melt the butter in a small saucepan, add the chopped leeks and garlic, cook gently for 5 minutes, add the potato and cook for a further 4–5 minutes.

4. Add the lamb mince, curry powder, chilli and cook for 2 minutes to brown the meat, pop a lid on and cook slowly for 15 minutes, stirring from time to time so the mixture doesn't stick to the pan. Add the coriander, peas and season with a bit of salt and pepper, then leave to cool.

5. Pre-heat the oven to 200°C and lightly grease a baking tray.

6. Divide the filling into 4 and pile onto one side of the pastry circles. Brush around the edges with egg and fold the circle over and press to create a tight seal. Crimp the edges neatly and brush them all over with egg.

7. Place the pasties on the greased baking sheet and bake for 15 minutes, reduce the oven to 180°C and cook for 20 minutes more until golden brown. Serve hot or cold. I love them with a little mint sauce drizzled over even though they are spicy.

Curry Roasted Butternut Squash

This curry roasted butternut squash is a wonderful way to cook this versatile vegetable. Imparting tons of flavour into the squash and using the sugar gives a beautiful caramelisation to the flesh and helps to firm it up so that it won't turn to mush when you add it to other dishes. Use any curry mix you like; here, I have used Kashmiri for a real punch, but you choose, and make it as hot or mild as you prefer.

serves 4

1 large butternut squash
2 tablespoons soft, dark, brown sugar
2 teaspoon Kashmiri spice mix or your personal favourite
pinch of sea salt flakes
pinch of black pepper

1.   Before you begin, line a baking tray with a sheet of greaseproof paper and preheat the oven to 180°C.

2.   Using a sharp knife, carefully cut the squash in half and scoop out the seeds. Then, score through the squash length and crossways, taking care not to cut through the skin; you want the squash to remain intact.

3.   Rub 1 tablespoon of sugar into each side; as you rub, the sugar will start to melt and pour into the grooves you have just cut. Sift 1 teaspoon of the spice mix over each half in an even layer. Finally, sprinkle each half with salt and pepper.

4.   Put the squash onto the baking sheet and pop it into the centre of the oven and roast for about an hour or until the squash is tender and the surface caramelised.

5.   Remove from the oven and use in your favourite recipes. Mine is in a curry or even a side dish for a curry or any other spicy food. Cold curried squash is delicious in a salad too.

Hot and Spicy

Though much is said here in the book about favourite Yorkshire recipes, traditional foods, sweets, cakes and the like, another huge favourite, and one that employs over 100,000 people and is a vital billion-pound industry for the region, is curry. For six years in a row, Bradford was crowned the Curry Capital of Britain and most certainly deserved the accolade for the city where once wool was king.

Just why Bradford became so renowned for curry is simple, according to Nick Ahad in an article for the once tourist agency Welcome to Yorkshire. When the wool industry was booming, the factories needed staff. So adverts asked for (cheap) labour, and they came from present-day India, Pakistan, and Bangladesh. But as Nick points out, Yorkshire's 1960s meat-and-two-veg diet was not to their liking. No wonder then, that since the mills and their clatter of looms have fallen silent, the aroma of exotic spices has become synonymous with the city.

However, curry is everywhere in the county, not just Bradford, with styles from across the Indian subcontinent and beyond, and there are over 200 curry houses in Yorkshire if you want to eat in or take away. Or, as I love to cook curry in my house, all the spices needed to cook curry at home are so easy to find, as are the many other ingredients required. A favourite place of mine to shop for these is Kirkgate Market in Leeds, one of the largest in Europe when it opened in 1857. The market was designed by architect Joseph Paxton, who also designed Crystal Palace in London, and was where Marks and Spencer started life in 1884, then called Marks' Penny Bazaar.

If you can't make it to Leeds, there are many retailers in Yorkshire and, of course, online to use; see page 197 for the ones I like.

My Favourite Dhal

I cannot remember the source of this recipe as I have used it for quite some time and have tinkered around with it. The dhal is my comfort food, and, crazy as it may sound, I am known to eat it for breakfast following a recommendation once by an Ayurvedic doctor in Sri Lanka. This recipe makes simple, tasty dhal. Feel free to add to it as you like.

serves 6

210 g black lentils, soaked overnight in cold water
4 tablespoons butter
1 large onion, finely chopped
200 ml tinned tomatoes, chopped
2 garlic cloves, crushed
½ tablespoon fresh ginger, peeled and finely grated
1 small cinnamon stick
1 teaspoon chilli powder
1 teaspoon ground cumin
1 teaspoon ground turmeric
2 tablespoons tomato puree
750 ml water
sea salt
75 ml single cream
small mint leaves and thick plain yoghurt to garnish

1.   Drain the lentils through a colander, rinse with cold water and put to one side.

2.   In a large saucepan or ovenproof casserole, melt 3 tablespoons of butter over medium heat. Add the onions and cook for 5 minutes until soft but not browning. Add the chopped tomato, garlic, ginger, cinnamon, chilli, cumin and turmeric to the pan. Stir well and cook for 3 minutes still on medium heat. Add the tomato puree and stir well.

3.   Add the water, stir well and bring to a gentle boil. Cook for 15 minutes. Add the lentils, cover with a lid, and cook slowly and gently for up to 2 hours or until the lentils are soft. Check occasionally to make sure the water has not boiled dry, add more if needed.

4.   Once cooked, remove the cinnamon, season generously with sea salt, add the cream and remaining butter, and stir.

5.   Serve in warm bowls garnished with mint and thick yoghurt if you like, plus I love to eat this with soft, warm roti.

Classic Game Terrine

An excellent way to eat Yorkshire game. Use a mixture of meats such as pheasant or pigeon breast, lean venison, saddle of hare or rabbit.

serves 8

25 g breadcrumbs
3 tablespoons parsley, finely chopped
pinch dried thyme
1 teaspoon mace
425 g good quality sausage meat
2 cloves garlic, finely chopped
1 egg, beaten

125 ml port
sea salt and freshly ground
    black pepper
350 g streaky bacon
2 tablespoons vegetable oil
900 g chunks of lean mixed
    game meat

1. Mix the breadcrumbs, parsley, thyme and mace in a large mixing bowl.

2. Add the sausage meat, garlic, egg, and port to the bowl. Season with a good pinch of salt and plenty of black pepper.

3. Flatten the bacon rashers using the back of a knife and line a 1-kilo terrine dish leaving any excess length hanging over the sides.

4. Heat the oil to medium-hot and cook the game quickly for 2 minutes to brown lightly.

5. Divide the sausage meat mix into 3 and place one-third across the bottom of the terrine, top with a layer of game and repeat with the sausage mix and game. Finish with a top layer of sausage meat. Place one into the bottom of the terrine dish.

6. Preheat the oven to 160°C. Fold the hanging strips of bacon over the sausage meat and cover the top with a double layer of foil to seal.

7. Stand the terrine in a deep roasting tin in the centre of the oven. Half fill with boiling water and cook for 1½ hours or until an internal temperature of 85°C, or pierce with a metal skewer which should come out very hot.

8. Remove from the oven and place on a baking tray. To compress the terrine, place a piece of cardboard wrapped in foil to fit just inside the rim of the terrine. Weight down with heavy tins or a brick. Leave for several hours or, even better, overnight.

9. Serve with pickles, cornichons, a side salad, and crusty bread. Will keep for up to a week in the fridge.

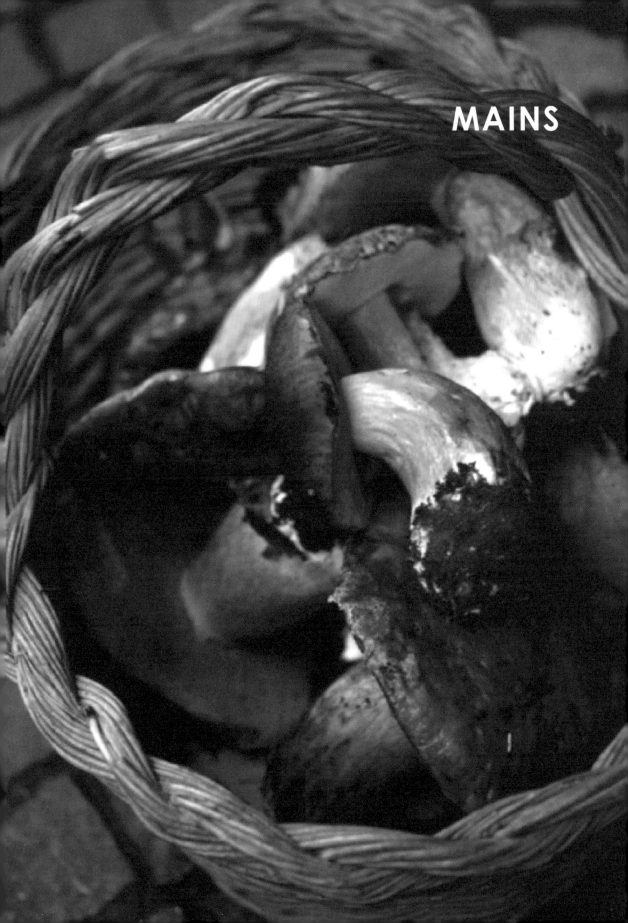

MAINS

Fish IN Chips

I would love to take credit for this innovative recipe of fat goujons of haddock wrapped in potato and then quickly deep-fried, but that honour goes to The Chef's Table team at True Foods in North Yorkshire. We loved it so much that we worked to replicate it at home.

Though it doesn't quite match the meticulous presentation when the chefs put it together, we love our version and will cook it regularly instead of eating a traditional plate full of fish and chips.

You will need a spiraliser to make this. I can't think of any other way of making the potato thin enough. Use fresh haddock or cod, and take care not to cut the fish too thick, or it will not cook through before the potato starts to burn in the hot fat.

serves 2

1 litre vegetable oil
300 g thick haddock or cod
500 g large red potatoes, peeled
2 tablespoons flour
sea salt and pepper

1. Put the oil into a large pan or wok and put it on low heat to start the warming while preparing the potatoes and fish.

2. Cut the fish into four equal chunky 'fingers'. Put to one side. Then spiralise the potatoes carefully to create long strands the thickness of spaghetti. Keep the strands to one side but do not wash or cover with water.

3. Mix the flour with a good pinch of salt and pepper on a deep plate. Raise the heat under the oil; you are looking to achieve a temperature of 170°C to fry the fish.

4. While the oil is heating, take each chunk of fish, and dip it into the flour, making sure it is completely coated. Once coated, wrap long strands of potato first lengthways, then a few more around the fish to enclose it. Repeat with the other pieces of fish.

5. Check the temperature of the oil. It is imperative it is not too hot, or the potato will burn before the fish is cooked. Carefully slide in two pieces of fish. Cook, turning the fish constantly for about five minutes or until the potato starts to turn a deep (not dark) brown. Lift out with a slotted spoon and keep warm while cooking the other two pieces.

6. Serve at once with mushy or garden peas and a wedge of lemon.

Ron's Favourite Curry

My husband has become a great cook recently, and I love watching him as he works; he is far more organised than I will ever be. He is meticulous in his preparation and carefully measures everything into ramekin dishes and bowls, all in the order they appear in the recipe – a great way to cook, especially if there are lots of ingredients.

One of the dishes he cooks that we all love is this curry which is not his invention but came originally from The Seafood Shack by Kirsty Scobie and Fenella Renwick. He cooked the recipe faithfully from their award-winning book but has refined it to what we have more readily available and adjusted certain ingredients more to our liking.

serves 4

500 g thick Whitby cod fillet
3 tablespoons vegetable oil
2 red onions, roughly chopped
1 white onion, sliced
1 red chilli, thinly chopped
2 garlic cloves, finely chopped
1 cm ginger, peeled and finely chopped
2 sweet pointed red peppers, de-seeded and thinly sliced
2 tablespoons Thai red curry paste
2 tablespoons tomato puree
1 teaspoon cayenne pepper
2 teaspoons ground cumin
1 fish stock cube, crumbled
2 tablespoons runny honey
2 x 400 g tins chopped tomatoes
1 x 400 ml tin coconut milk
2 tablespoons Thai fish sauce
2 tablespoons sweet chilli sauce
2 tablespoons soy sauce
1 lime, quartered
salt to taste
garnish:
1 tablespoon full-fat crème fraiche
small handful mange tout, finely shredded
4 spring onions, finely chopped

1. Cut the cod into 4 cm chunks and set them aside. Heat a large, deep pan or stockpot on medium heat; add 2 tablespoons of oil, the onions, chilli, garlic, ginger and peppers. Sweat everything down until the onions are caramelised – about 10 minutes.

2. Stir in the red curry paste, tomato puree, cayenne pepper, cumin, and crumbled fish stock cube, and then add the honey. Cook this off for 5 minutes until the smell of the spices comes through, stirring occasionally.

3. Add the tomatoes, coconut milk, fish sauce, sweet chilli and soy sauces. Squeeze and add in the lime. Cook on a low simmer for 15 to 20 minutes to thicken up your sauce. Add a bit of salt if needed. Stir every 5 minutes to stop it from burning on the bottom.

4. Using a non-stick frying pan, heat the remaining oil to super-hot. Fry the cod until it's lightly browned all over.

5. Add the fish to the curry sauce, and simmer very gently for another 5 minutes until it's just cooked through; take care not to cook too long, or the fish will turn rubbery.

6. Serve with rice to soak up the sauce, soft pitta or roti with the garnish in bowls on the side.

Cantonese Ginger Fish

Super easy and packed with wonderful flavours have made this recipe hugely popular in my busy household for many years. The recipe is in my stash of much-loved recipes and comes from a cookbook I once owned, and I apologise that I can't remember which.

Choose lovely meaty fish such as fresh Whitby cod or haddock for this dish and serve simply with jasmine rice.

serves 4

4 x 180 g skin-on fish fillets
3 tablespoons dark soy sauce
1 tablespoon sesame oil
2 tablespoons Chinese rice wine (or dry sherry)
1 tablespoon granulated sugar
5 cm fresh ginger, peeled, cut into matchsticks
1 bird's eye red chilli, deseeded and finely sliced
3 spring onions, finely sliced
3 tablespoons coriander, leaves only, chopped

1. Gently wash the fish in cold water and dry with kitchen paper. Pop the fillets, skin side up onto a heatproof dish or deep plate that will fit into a steamer then put to one side.

2. Mix the soy, sesame oil, rice wine and sugar and pour over the fish. Scatter the ginger, chilli and half the spring onions over the fish and steam for 8–10 minutes, until the flesh parts easily when pierced with a knife.

3. Transfer the fish to warmed dinner plates and strain the juices over the top. Scatter with the remaining spring onions and coriander and serve with jasmine rice.

Quick and Easy Lemon Sardine Pasta

One product I never thought I would see made in Yorkshire was pasta. Thanks to the hardworking, innovative young company named quite simply Yorkshire Pasta, we now have our very own made here in the county using flour sourced from a local mill. And it is excellent.

The pasta is vegetarian and vegan friendly as it contains no egg. The pasta shapes are cut using traditional bronze dies, which give the pasta a slightly roughened surface making it even better for holding onto the pasta sauce.

Here I use linguine. You can, of course, use your favourite pasta brand in this recipe, or the tortiglioni from this exciting company is good too; you can find their details on page 197.

serves 4

400 g linguine pasta
3 tablespoons extra virgin olive oil
1 tablespoon shallot, finely chopped
2 teaspoons chilli flakes
1 garlic clove, finely chopped
200 g of tinned, boneless sardine fillets, drained
1 lemon, zest and juice
1 tablespoon flat-leaf parsley, chopped
2 tablespoons baby kale
sea salt flakes and freshly ground white pepper

1. Cook the linguine according to the package instructions. Drain but keep back 2 tablespoons of the cooking water in the pan. Toss the pasta in the pan and add 1 tablespoon of olive oil. Keep warm.

2. Make the sauce while the pasta is cooking. Heat the remaining olive oil in a large heavy-bottomed frying pan to hot but not smoking, add the shallot and cook for 1 minute, add the chilli flakes, stir, lower the heat slightly and add the garlic. Stir well and cook for 1 minute.

3. Add the sardines to the frying pan and stir taking care not to break them up too much. Finally, add the lemon zest and stir again.

4. Tip the cooked linguine into a warmed serving bowl, stir through the sardine sauce, parsley and baby kale (the heat of the pasta and the sauce will be enough to cook the tiny leaves). Add salt and pepper to taste. Finish with a drizzle of lemon juice and serve immediately.

Lime Caramelised Salmon Salad

serves 6–8

100 g soft brown sugar
120 ml water
2.5 cm fresh ginger, peeled and finely diced
2 garlic cloves, crushed
1 red chilli, seeds removed, finely sliced
4 tablespoons fish sauce
4 tablespoons lime juice
4 x 175 g salmon fillets
175 g bean sprouts
85 g fresh mint leaves
50 g fresh coriander leaves
350 g mixed salad leaves
1 spring onion, finely sliced
2 tablespoons extra virgin olive oil
2 tablespoons salted peanuts
1 lime, quartered

1. Put the sugar and water into a saucepan and bring to a gentle boil, stirring. Once boiling, add the ginger, garlic and chilli. Stir and boil to reduce to a thick, glossy sauce. Once syrupy, add the fish sauce and lime juice. Stir and put to one side.

2. Lay the fresh salmon fillets on a sheet of kitchen paper. Check the salmon over for any small bones, taking care to remove them. Cut the fillets into 2.5 cm cubes and put them into a bowl. Spoon over the sauce and stir gently. Put to one side while you prepare the salad.

3. Place the bean sprouts in a large bowl and pour over a pint of boiling water. Drain and then put to one side. Pick over the herbs and salad leaves to make sure they are clean, place in a large salad bowl and mix thoroughly. Add the chopped onion and the bean sprouts.

4. Heat the olive oil in a non-stick frying pan until hot but not smoking. Add the salmon pieces coated in the sauce and fry in the hot oil for 5 minutes whilst moving the fish pieces around the pan with a spatula to prevent them from sticking and burning. Once cooked, remove from the pan and keep warm. Add any remaining marinade to the frying pan and stir well over medium heat to warm through.

5. Divide the salad into 4 bowls, lay the fish on the salad. Lightly crush the peanuts in a pestle and mortar and scatter over the dishes. Spoon the warm sauce over the fish and serve at once with the lime quarters and rice if desired.

Pancit

Pancit is everyday fare in the Philippines, and a noodle dish can be made with vegetables, seafood, meat, or all three together. Unfortunately, the noodles in the dish are also called pancit, which makes it a little confusing, but any good Asian supermarket will be able to help choose the right ones.

This recipe uses the pancit canton type noodles as they are the easiest to work with and ones which are possibly the most familiar. If you are stuck, use Chinese egg noodles about the thickness of fresh spaghetti.

Here I am using prawns, but feel free to add meat if you prefer, or make with only vegetables and any you would usually stir fry will work well – peppers, pak choi, shredded cabbage, spring onion, and mushrooms are excellent.

serves 4

4 tablespoons vegetable oil
250 g mixed vegetables, chopped
1 onion, thinly sliced
2 cloves garlic, peeled and finely chopped
2 cm ginger, peeled and finely grated
125 g small, peeled prawns
600 ml chicken stock
250 g dried pancit canton noodles
2 tablespoons soy sauce
1 tablespoon fish sauce
small handful of coriander leaves only

1. Heat the oil in a large wok or a deep-frying pan. Add the chopped vegetables and onion, fry for 3 minutes over high heat. Add the garlic and fry for 1 minute more.

2. Add the ginger and the prawns and continue to cook until the prawns have turned pink and are cooked through; this will only take a few minutes.

3. Add the stock and bring to a steady boil, then add the noodles. Stir gently to help soften the noodles, reduce the heat and add the soy and the fish sauce. Cook for 5–8 minutes for the noodles to soak up some but not all the stock.

4. To serve: spoon out the noodles, prawns and vegetables into warmed bowls, then spoon over the broth. Garnish with finely chopped coriander, if you wish.

BBQ Rib Eye Steak, Grilled Asparagus and Teriyaki Sauce

serves 2

for the teriyaki sauce
75 ml soy sauce
75 ml mirin, Japanese sweet rice wine
75 ml sake
1 tablespoon sugar
the remaining recipe:
2 x 150 g rib-eye steaks
2 tablespoons vegetable oil
sea salt and black pepper
1 x 250 g packet of local asparagus, trimmed of woody ends
pinch of togarashi seasoning (or cayenne pepper) (optional)
white and black sesame seeds to serve (optional)

1. To make the teriyaki sauce, combine all ingredients in a saucepan. Stir the mixture well. Put it on medium heat and bring to a boil. Turn the heat down to low and simmer for a couple of minutes. Then, stop the heat and cool the mixture. It's now ready to use, or store the sauce in a clean bottle in the fridge

2. Heat a griddle pan until hot. Rub the steaks with a little oil, salt and pepper and griddle cook for 2 minutes on each side to be medium to rare. Remove from the pan and leave to rest.

3. While the beef is resting, rub the asparagus with the remaining oil, then lay on the griddle and grill for 2–3 minutes, turning now and then until they start to soften but still have a bite and have tiny char marks on them.

4. Divide the asparagus between two plates. Carve the steaks into 1 cm strips and lay on top of the asparagus, pouring over the meat juices left from resting. Cover each steak with a few tablespoons of teriyaki sauce and sprinkle with the togarashi if using, or sesame seeds.

Recipe and image courtesy of British Asparagus

Corned Beef Hash

When you need a nourishing and comforting dish, little comes as close as a traditional corned beef hash. This recipe is so simple to make and packs flavour and comfort by the bucketload.

serves 4

4 tablespoons butter
2 large onions, peeled and finely sliced
450 g red potatoes, washed and unpeeled, cut into 1 cm cubes
2 large carrots, peeled and cut into 1 cm cubes
700 ml hot beef stock
400 g corned beef, cut into 1 cm cubes
4 tablespoons Worcestershire sauce
2 tablespoons wholegrain mustard
4 tablespoons garden peas, frozen

1. Heat the butter on medium heat in a large pan or casserole dish. Add the onions and cook until they are melting and soft and just about to start turning brown.

2. Add the potatoes and carrots to the pan and stir thoroughly, if there isn't enough butter to coat them, add a little more. Cook gently for 5 minutes, stirring from time to time. Add the beef stock, bring to a gentle boil, reduce the heat to low and cook for a further 3 minutes.

3. Add the corned beef cubes, Worcestershire sauce, mustard and cook for 20 minutes, stirring carefully with a spoon from time to time. From now on, take care not to over stir the hash or both the corned beef and potatoes will break up, try to keep them as intact as possible during the cooking.

4. Once ready keep the hash over a low heat, add the frozen peas and stir through. Divide the hash between four hot plates and serve immediately. We love the hash with a dollop of brown sauce and a fried egg on top.

The Ultimate Chilli

This is the ultimate chilli recipe, at least according to my husband, the aficionado in this house, given it is not my thing!

He found the recipe some years ago in a *BBC Good Food* magazine and, over time, has adapted it to his liking; he especially prefers blade steak as the meat of choice, much preferring the texture, taste and tenderness when cooked.

serves 6

the spice mix:
2 teaspoons black peppercorns
2 tablespoons cumin seeds
2 tablespoons coriander seeds
2 medium red chillies
the meat:
3 tablespoons vegetable oil
1½ kg blade steak, cut into large chunks
2 onions, finely chopped
3 garlic cloves, finely chopped
2 tablespoons tomato puree
1 tablespoon smooth peanut butter
½ teaspoon instant espresso coffee powder
2 tablespoons apple cider vinegar
1 litre beef or chicken stock
2 bay leaves
small piece of cinnamon stick
pinch of salt
2 tablespoons semolina
25 g 60–70% dark chocolate, grated
400 g can kidney beans, drained (optional)

1. Make the spice mix: heat a large frying pan to hot, add the peppercorns, cumin and coriander seeds and toast until you can smell the spicy aromas; this will be seconds rather than minutes. Tip them into a spice grinder or pestle and mortar and grind to a fine powder. Throw the chillies into the same hot pan and roast on both sides for about a minute. Put to one side.

2. Heat a large cast-iron (or similar) casserole dish to hot, add 2 tablespoons of the oil, then add chunks of beef several at a time without crowding and sear all over for a few minutes. Remove and keep to one side. Continue until all the meat is seared, adding a little more oil if needed.

3. Put the onions into the same casserole and cook until soft and just

starting to colour, about 5–6 minutes. Add the garlic, stir and cook for 1 minute.

4. Heat oven to 140°C.

5. Tip the meat and any juices into the pan with the onions and garlic, and add the spice powder, tomato puree, peanut butter and the coffee. Give it a big stir making sure everything is coated, then add the vinegar and beef or chicken stock.

6. Add the toasted chillies, bay leaves, cinnamon and salt, give another good stir, then bring to a gentle boil. Cover with the lid and put into the centre of the oven and cook for 3 hours. Check from time to time that the chilli is cooking slowly, as cooking too fast can make the meat tough. The chilli is ready when the meat is tender and about to fall apart.

7. Remove from the oven, uncover and simmer on the stove for 5 minutes. Add the semolina and simmer for 2–3 minutes. Stir through the grated chocolate, then add the beans (if using) and cook for a couple of minutes to heat the beans through.

8. Rest the chilli for 15 minutes and before serving remove the whole chillies. Serve with warm tortillas, guacamole, and sour cream.

Kitchen Notes:

You can leave the chilli to cool down and keep in the fridge until the next day, when it will taste even better, though that is hard to imagine.

Shoulder of Lamb Casserole

A much-overlooked joint of meat is a shoulder of lamb; I have no idea why as it is cheaper than many other cuts of lamb and is perfect for long slow cooking, which I love.

serves 6

6 tablespoons vegetable oil
1.2 kg boned, rolled shoulder of lamb
3 tablespoons plain flour, seasoned with a bit of salt and pepper
1 large onion, peeled and cut into large chunks
220 g baby carrots, scrubbed
1 leek, finely sliced
2 garlic cloves, peeled
1 glass of red wine
1 litre lamb or beef stock
2 bay leaves
few sprigs of flat-leaf parsley, finely chopped
1 small sprig of rosemary
2 tablespoons Worcestershire sauce (optional)
1 tablespoon flour
1 tablespoon butter
sea salt and black pepper

1. Heat the oven to 150°C.

2. Heat the vegetable oil in a large casserole to hot and sear the shoulder of lamb on all sides.

2. Put the lamb on a large plate, sprinkle over the seasoned flour and leave to one side.

3. Put all the vegetables into the same casserole you seared the lamb in. Stir to coat in the oil and meat juices and cook for 2 minutes. Tip them onto the plate with the lamb.

4. Turn up the heat, add the wine and stir to scrape up any bits on the bottom of the pan. Cook until the wine is but a glaze on the bottom of the pan. Add one-third of the stock and stir again.

5. Return the lamb and vegetables to the casserole, add the herbs and Worcestershire sauce (if using) and the remaining stock, cover and put into the oven, and leave to cook for 6 hours.

6. After the casserole is cooked, check the gravy; if it is too thin, pour it through a sieve into a saucepan and heat gently.

7. Make a paste from the plain flour and butter. Bring the gravy to a boil

and whisk in small pieces of the butter paste thoroughly; the gravy will become thick and glossy.

8.   Taste the gravy and adjust the seasoning to your taste with sea salt and black pepper. Add the gravy back to the casserole dish and simmer on top of the stove for 5 minutes.

9.   Lift out the lamb carefully; it will be very tender and starting to fall apart.

10.   To serve, all you need to do is pull the meat into chunks, serve on hot plates with mashed potatoes, gravy and the cooked vegetables poured over the top.

Kitchen Notes: You can make this the day before, cool it and reheat it when needed, and though it is hard to believe, it will taste even better.

Braised Pork Shoulder with Rhubarb

Pork is such a wonderful meat, and one of my favourite cooking methods is braising. This braised pork recipe combines the pork with rhubarb, a delicious accompaniment to any fatty meat. This pork recipe produces lots of juices which make a lovely sauce.

serves 4

1.5 kg pork shoulder, on the bone
4 large shallots, peeled
6 garlic cloves, peeled
5 cm fresh ginger, peeled and grated
3 tablespoons honey
1 teaspoon freshly ground pepper
2 tablespoons extra virgin olive oil
2 red chillies
500 ml dry cider
500 g rhubarb, trimmed weight
1 teaspoon ice-cold butter, chopped into tiny pieces

1. Preheat the oven to 180°C. Score the skin of the pork with a very sharp knife, then put it into a large, roomy roasting tray.

2. Put the shallots, garlic, ginger, honey, pepper and olive oil into a food processor and blitz to form a thick paste. Smear the paste all over the pork including the skin.

3. Snap the chillies in half and throw them into the roasting tray, and pour in the cider. Cover tightly with foil and roast for 2 hours.

4. Take the dish from the oven and raise the temperature to 220°C. Cut the rhubarb into 7 cm lengths and scatter into the sauce. Return to the oven uncovered, cook for 20 minutes.

5. Remove the pork from the oven and place it to one side to rest for at least 10 minutes before slicing. Strain the pan juices through a fine sieve into a small saucepan. Keep the rhubarb to one side.

6. Place the sauce over high heat and reduce by one third. Drop a few pieces of the ice-cold butter into the sauce, and over medium heat, shake until all the butter has melted, repeat until all the butter is used up and the sauce is glossy.

7. Slice the pork (it will not make neat slices, but don't worry, this is quite a rustic dish), place on a serving plate topped with the rhubarb and serve with the sauce. The pork is also lovely cold, pulled from the bone and made into a salad or a sandwich.

Meat, Game and Charcuterie in Yorkshire

How different the landscape of Yorkshire would look were it not for the animals that have grazed there for hundreds of years, if not longer. The lush Dales without grazing sheep are unthinkable; their presence is as much a landmark as the dry-stone walls crisscrossing the hills.

Throughout Yorkshire, the diversity of the landscape means a wide range of meat, poultry and game are readily available. There are, of course, all the usual meats, beef, lamb, pork et al. and many specialist ones too, such as the famous Nidderdale lamb, Wagyu beef from the east of Yorkshire, venison in the west, and even water buffalo in the south.

Up in North Yorkshire, the heather-covered moors are renowned worldwide for high-quality feathered game. The shoots over the winter are estimated to bring over £100 million a year to the Yorkshire economy. And again, game conservation has also shaped the landscape of the moors and uplands. The abundance of game makes it a relatively cheap yet healthy meat to buy, and as it freezes so well, can be eaten year-round.

The growing and buying of ethical, sustainably grown, and heritage breeds have grown exponentially in recent years. For this, we have to thank our many, many farmers, butchers and farm shops for the work they do in both supporting and communicating this move. Not long ago, butchers were in decline, and not just in Yorkshire. What a delight it is that this has now changed; I have three butchers alone near where I live, all excellent. Make friends with yours; they are a fount of knowledge regarding what to buy or how to cook it.

For many years, the trend for the more continental style of cured meats has been on the rise and is now firmly fixed. Where once a York ham or a piece of haslet was about as fancy as it got, now butchers are curing salamis, chorizo, bresaola, guanciale and much more in-house. Chris Wildman of Town End Farm Shop in Malhamdale bucked the trend with his award-winning charcuterie, including Yorkshire Chorizo. Another early adopter was award-winning Lishman's in Ilkley, where father David and daughter Emma working together became British Charcuterie Champion producers. They are now as renowned for their cured meats as their traditional butchery, famous pies and hams.

I mention just a few of the fantastic farmers, butchers, farm shops, and food halls found in Yorkshire. However, there are many more. You can find some of my favourites and organisations to help you in the supplier list at the end of the book (page 196).

Lamb Cooked in a Blanket

For a perfect roast leg of lamb, one of the best ways to cook it is in a blanket. This may seem an odd way to cook any meat, but it is based on an old method of cooking when the meat would have long, slow cooking wrapped in hay.

I was first taught this cooking method when I lived in France and, nervously, I gave it a try and was astonished that it produced the juiciest, most tender roast lamb I had ever eaten. Having now cooked it this way many times, I assure you that you will not be disappointed.

Buy local lamb with the bone in and get your butcher to trim and tie the lamb ready for the oven. I like to buy my lamb from a local farm shop where its provenance is assured.

serves 6–8

2 kg leg of lamb, on the bone
3 garlic cloves, sliced
2 tablespoons extra virgin olive oil
sea salt and black pepper
4 sprigs of fresh rosemary
for the gravy:
125 ml red wine
500 ml beef stock
1 tablespoon plain flour
1 tablespoon butter, softened

If your meat has been in the refrigerator, remove it for at least 1 hour before cooking.

1.   Heat the oven to 230°C.

2.   Place the leg of lamb on a chopping board, skin side up. Using a sharp knife, make approximately 20 tiny slits into and under the skin, taking care not to cut into the meat. Slide a slice of garlic into each slit.

3.   Place the lamb, skin side up, into a large roasting tin and rub the olive oil all over the surface. Sprinkle generously with sea salt and black pepper and place uncovered in the hot oven for 55 minutes. The oven's heat will cause the fat to spit; there may also be some smoke but be assured this is quite normal.

4.   Remove the lamb from the oven; take care as the tin and the meat will be very hot, and the fat may still be spitting. Lay the rosemary sprigs on the lamb and immediately wrap the tin with 3 layers of foil. Then, cover the whole package with a thick blanket or several large, thick bath towels.

5. Place the package somewhere warm but not hot and leave for 6 (for rare) or 8 hours (for medium-rare to medium). The lamb continues to cook slowly in its thick wrapping using the residual heat and steam from the meat, bone and roasting tin. As it cooks slowly, the lamb softens and releases lots of juices to use later for the gravy.

6. After your chosen time, unwrap the lamb and remove it from the roasting tin onto a carving board and cover again with the foil.

7. Make the gravy by placing the roasting tin over high heat; add the red wine and stir well once the juices are bubbling. Cook for 5 minutes, add the stock and turn the heat down. Leave the sauce to reduce and thicken.

8. Meanwhile, mix the flour and butter to form a paste. Once the sauce has thickened slightly, turn up the heat, add the flour paste, and whisk until all the flour is absorbed and the sauce has thickened. Season with salt and pepper to taste, then strain into a warmed gravy jug.

9. Carve the lamb and serve at once onto hot plates with a bit of gravy and fresh seasonal vegetables.

10. If the lamb is too undercooked for your liking, put the lamb slices into a hot oven for a few minutes but no longer than 5 minutes or the lamb will start to tighten up and become tough.

Spicy Goat Stew

Goat is lovely, lean meat and when slow-cooked, produces a rich, flavourful dish. Goat is available from many good butchers and online; I buy mine from a local farm shop. This goat recipe gives a wonderful, warm spicy flavour to the tender chunks of meat, making a terrific autumn or winter supper dish. Serve with grilled flatbreads or plain boiled rice to soak up the lovely sauce.

serves 4

roasted spice mix:
1 tablespoon cumin seeds
½ tablespoon caraway seeds
1 tablespoon fennel seeds
4 cloves
½ tablespoon cardamom seeds
3 tablespoons ras-el-hanout spice
  mix
stew:
900 g goat shoulder, cut into large
  chunks
180 ml yoghurt

small handful of fresh mint leaves,
  roughly chopped
2 cloves garlic, crushed
55 g butter
6 tablespoons vegetable oil
2 medium red onions, finely
  chopped
2 tablespoons ginger, freshly grated
3 tablespoons roasted spice mix
2 tablespoons tomato paste
750 ml beef stock
handful of fresh coriander, leaves
  only

1. Mix all the spices together in a small bowl. Heat a large frying pan, sprinkle the spice mix in and cook for one minute, shaking the pan constantly. Tip the spices onto a plate and leave to cool. Store in a jar until needed.

2. Dry the meat with kitchen paper, place into a bowl, add the yoghurt, mint, garlic and stir well. Cover with a tea towel, put in the fridge, and leave to marinate for a minimum of 3 hours; even better, overnight.

3. Heat the butter and 4 tablespoons of the oil in a heatproof casserole dish, add the onions and cook gently for 5 minutes until soft. Add the ginger, 3 tablespoons of spice mix and stir. Add the tomato paste and stir again.

4. Add the stock, bring to a boil, reduce and simmer for 15 minutes. Pour the sauce into a food processor and blend thoroughly. Pass through a fine sieve into a jug and keep to one side. Preheat the oven to 160°C.

5. Reheat the casserole dish on the stove, add the remaining oil and once hot, remove the meat from the marinade and add to the casserole and fry for 5 minutes until lightly browned. Pour the sauce over the meat, bring to a boil and cook for 5 minutes.

6. Cover the casserole with a lid and place it in the middle of the preheated oven. Cook for 4 hours, occasionally check it is not drying out, add boiling water if needed. The meat should be soft and tender when cooked. Check the seasoning and leave to stand for 10 minutes. Garnish with chopped coriander.

Chicken Marbella

This is an iconic chicken dish first published back in 1982; a dish that fell out of favour but is making something of a comeback. This is no surprise as it is not only super-easy to make, but also delicious with its careful balance of sweetness from the sugar and prunes, the acidity of the vinegar and saltiness from olives and capers. There's a long marinate overnight so you will need to plan that in, then all that is left is to pop it in the oven to bake. Easy.

serves 4

pinch sea salt and freshly ground
    black pepper
6 skinless and boneless free-range
    chicken thighs
3 garlic cloves, finely chopped
4 tablespoons red wine vinegar
2 tablespoons brine from the olives
120 ml dry white wine
1 tablespoon of soft brown sugar
100 g green olives in brine, pitted
180 g pitted prunes
60 g of caper berries
2 tablespoons extra virgin olive oil

1. Sprinkle the salt and a few good grinds of black pepper onto your chopping board and press the chicken thighs down into the salt and pepper, then roll each thigh tight and lay in a bowl.

2. In another small bowl mix the garlic, vinegar, brine, wine and sugar and lightly whisk. Add the olives, prunes and capers, stir then pour over the chicken thighs. Cover the dish tightly with clingfilm or wax wrap and place into the fridge to marinate overnight.

3. Preheat the oven to 170°C.

4. When ready to cook, lift the thighs from the dish and dry on kitchen paper.

5. Heat the oil in a frying pan until hot but not smoking. Add the thighs and sear all over until golden brown and slightly crisp.

6. Pack the browned thighs into a shallow ovenproof baking dish, pour over the marinade including olives, prunes and capers. Bake in the centre of the preheated oven for 45 minutes, basting the chicken with the marinade from time to time. The marinade will reduce, and the chicken turns dark golden and slightly caramelised.

7. Serve while piping hot with extra olives and capers and rice, or a mixture of rice and quinoa.

Moroccan-Inspired Chicken with Lentils and Pomegranate

serves 2–4

4 tablespoons vegetable oil
2 large skin-on chicken breasts
1 large onion, peeled and finely chopped
1 tablespoon fresh ginger, peeled and grated
3 garlic cloves, crushed
3 heaped teaspoons Moroccan spice blend mix (ras-el-hanout is good)
115 g red lentils, washed
115 g organic dried apricots, finely chopped
juice of 1 lemon
1litre hot chicken stock
large handful fresh mint, roughly chopped
large handful coriander leaves, chopped plus extra for garnish
large handful fresh pomegranate seeds for garnish

1. Heat the oil to medium-hot in a deep frying pan. Add the chicken breasts and cook for 3 minutes each side until golden brown all over. Lower the heat. Remove the chicken, put on kitchen paper and keep to one side.

2. In the same frying pan, add the chopped onion and cook for 5 minutes on low heat, taking care not to burn.

3. Add the grated ginger and garlic and cook for a further 3 minutes.

4. Raise the heat slightly, add the spices and stir well. Return the chicken to the pan. Add the lentils, apricots, lemon juice and ¾ of the hot stock, lower the heat and cook on a gentle simmer for 20 minutes, stirring occasionally. Add more hot stock if the mixture becomes too thick.

5. Add the mint and coriander and cook for another 10 minutes. Remove from the heat and leave to stand for a few minutes. Check that the stew isn't too thick; add a little more stock or hot water if it is.

6. Serve the chicken and sauce sprinkled with a little more chopped mint, coriander and pomegranate seeds.

Confit of Duck

Duck, particularly confit of duck, is very special to me as I have such fondness for the memories of the ducks and geese I used to have in France. The many happy hours, not just looking after them but often quietly sitting watching them, was one of the great joys of living there for me.

I had to quickly learn and accept the life cycle of keeping all the animals we had, and initially, I found it very hard, especially the first time one of the ducks was 'transformed', as I like to call it; I was terribly upset, and I also knew it had been silly to give them all names, and I never did that again.

So instead, I strove to give my little birds a happy life, they were entirely free-range and had huge areas to wander around in safely and with plenty to eat, and when 'that' time came, it was done swiftly and responsibly.

For the cooking, it was thanks to a special friendship I had formed in the village with Mme. Grande, the wife of our retired local plumber, I learned to use every scrap of meat and bone possible in making pâtés, terrines, rillettes, soups, and confit.

When I was first introduced to Mme. Grande she was 80 years old and an astonishing cook. She would ring me often when she was about to embark on some recipe or other, inviting me to cook alongside her as she taught me all her tips and tricks, how to prepare, cook, to preserve and store food; to make the most of the carcass and even the feathers.

But above all, she reminded me constantly what an honour it is to cook for family and friends. About the privilege and responsibility of raising animals and birds, growing vegetables and fruits, and not wasting a single scrap of food. Occasionally, there was a little local gossip too. She was remarkable, and I was extremely fond of her and forever grateful for what she taught me.

serves 2

2 large duck legs (about 400 g)
100 g coarse sea salt
1 teaspoon freshly ground black pepper
1 tablespoon fresh thyme
2 bay leaves
450 g duck or goose fat, melted
12 black peppercorns

1. Sprinkle salt, ground black pepper, and thyme all over the duck legs. Place into a heavy pot and tuck in the bay leaves. Cover and store in the fridge overnight.

2. The next day, preheat the oven to 130°C. Take the duck legs from the pot and keep the bay leaves. Clean off the salt, thyme, and pepper with a paper towel. Do not wash.

3. Wipe out the pot, put the legs back and pour over melted duck or goose fat to cover. Add the bay leaves and the peppercorns. Place in the centre of the oven and cook for 4 hours. The meat should be cooked through and starting to fall from the bone.

4. Once cooked, lift legs from duck fat onto a plate.

5. Strain the duck fat through a fine sieve or a coffee filter. Place duck legs into a clean Kilner jar and cover with duck fat. Close the lid, leave to cool, and then place into the refrigerator to allow fat to set. The confit can now be stored in the fridge for up to 6 months until needed.

6. When you are ready to eat it, gently warm the jar in hot water to soften the fat to reheat the confit. Lift duck legs from their fat, place them into a hot frying pan and cook for 3 to 4 minutes to crispen the skin, turning halfway through. Put onto a baking tray and place in a hot oven until heated right through, around 20 minutes.

Kitchen notes: My favourite way is how the French serve it, with sauté potatoes cooked in the fat from the jar (see the next page).

Sauté Potatoes

serves 4

450 g floury potatoes (Desiree, Estima, King Edward or Maris Piper)
250 g duck fat
Maldon salt (optional)

1. Peel the potatoes. Cut into generous 1 cm slices, then cut crossways into 1 cm cubes. Place the potato cubes into a colander and rinse under cold running water until the water runs clear.

2. Bring a large pan of water to a boil, add the potato cubes and cook for 2 minutes. Drain, then spread them onto either a clean kitchen towel or paper. Pat to dry thoroughly and leave to go cold.

3. Before cooking, line a large roasting tin with a paper towel and have a slotted spoon to hand.

4. In a large pot, melt the duck fat and heat to 190°C (if you don't have a thermometer, the fat is hot enough when you drop in a couple of cubes, and they sizzle and float to the surface).

5. Put roughly half the potato cubes into the hot fat; the temperature will drop slightly, so turn it up slightly. Let them sizzle and rise back to the surface, then cook for 2–3 minutes until they are just starting to brown; stir with the slotted spoon from time to time. Finally, scoop them up and lay them on the kitchen paper to drain and cool.

6. Wait for the fat temperature to rise again, add the remaining potato cubes and repeat. At this point, you can keep the potatoes before final cooking when you are ready to serve by covering them with a tea cloth and popping the tray into the fridge.

7. Once you are ready to serve, reheat the fat and prepare another dish with a paper towel.

8. Repeat as before, cooking the potato cubes in two lots. They will crispen up and turn golden within minutes, so keep an eye on them and as soon as they look like they are going from golden to dark, whip them out, drain them on the paper, then keep warm until you have cooked the rest.

9. Serve at once sprinkled with salt if you prefer. Enjoy.

Tandoori Chicken

This is something of a favourite hot spicy chicken dish that traditionally cooks in a tandoor oven which most of us don't have, but a regular oven does a pretty good job. If you have a ridged grill pan (or even better, use the barbecue), sear the meat to create those lovely black markings that look and taste good.

serves 4

marinating time: 12 hrs
4 skinless free-range chicken breasts

for the marinade:
4 tablespoons lemon juice, freshly squeezed
120 ml full-fat yoghurt
2 tablespoons vegetable oil
2 teaspoons garlic, finely chopped
2 teaspoons fresh ginger, peeled and finely chopped
2 tablespoons tomato puree
3 teaspoons unsmoked paprika
1 teaspoon ground cumin
1 teaspoon turmeric
1teaspoon garam masala, plus 1 teaspoon to use later
1 teaspoon sea salt
2–3 drops red food colouring, optional
garnish
lemon wedges and coriander leaves

1. Cut the chicken breasts into bite-sized chunks and pop them into a large resealable plastic bag.

2. Put all the marinade ingredients (keeping the extra garam masala to one side) into a food processor and whizz into a thick, smooth paste and the paprika has turned the marinade bright red; if not strong enough for your liking, add a few drops of food colouring.

3. Tip the marinade into the bag with the chicken, seal and gently massage to make sure the chicken is well coated; put them into the fridge, if possible, overnight, but for at least 6 hours.

4. Take the chicken from the fridge at least 20 minutes before you are ready to cook, as cooking the meat straight from the refrigerator will take longer, and the meat will be tough.

5. Preheat the oven to 180°C.

6. Optional: If you have a griddle pan, heat it slowly to hot but not burning and sear the chicken cubes to make lovely black markings before baking.

7. Place the chicken into an ovenproof dish. Cook in the middle of the oven for 20 minutes if you seared the chicken, or 25 minutes if not. Once cooked, take the dish from the oven and sprinkle with the extra garam masala. Put to one side for 5 minutes to rest the chicken.

8. Serve hot on basmati rice, garnished with coriander and lemon wedges.

Which chicken meat to use:

Breast meat is softer and quicker to cook; however, thigh and legs have a more robust flavour, so they stand up well to the spices and flavours.

Denby Dale and Pies

When we put our minds to it in Yorkshire, never be surprised at what can happen. An event at the tiny village of Denby Dale back in 1788 created enough of a sensation to capture the imagination of the national press, which in those days was something of a coup. The cause was nothing more than a very large pie. We love our pies in Yorkshire, they are part of our heritage, but until this moment, never quite on the scale of the 18th-century whopper. For the following 200-plus years the quirky tradition of making the world's largest pies has continued in Denby Dale, spreading the name of the village and the county worldwide.

Sadly, there is little evidence as to the precise size or weight of the 1788 pie. What is known is the pie was reputedly made to celebrate the (short-lived) return to sanity of King George III. The second giant pie baked in 1815, to celebrate Wellington's victory at Waterloo, reputedly contained at least 20 fowls and a couple of sheep.

There were a further nine giant pies, with the last made in 2012. This pie is well documented and was filled with meat supplied by nearby Farmer Copleys Farm Shop. This pie contained a staggering 435 kg local beef, 50 rabbits, 35 pigeons, 3 hares, 10 grouse, 36 chickens, 63 kg of turkey and 21 ducks. The pie weighed over 3 tonnes making it equivalent to almost 7,000 family-sized pies. And that was not even the biggest. That honour goes to the Millennium Pie weighing in at 12 tonnes.

Just why did the pretty, unassuming village tucked away between Wakefield, Huddersfield and Barnsley take on the mantle of building enormous pies? The question is open to much speculation involving local rivalries, royal connections, inflated egos and the rest. There is no secret though. The simplest and clearest answer is because they wanted to, and they could.

Easter Pie — the Yorkshire Version

One of the best-known Italian pies is the Easter pie. Like many Italian dishes that have gained popularity outside their home, you will find recipes for Easter pies in abundance, and everyone seems to have a variation.

Making my first Easter pie I stayed true to the Italian ingredients. However, given the abundance of talent and creativity here in Yorkshire, from sausage and charcuterie producers and the number of artisan cheeses, I can proudly say most of the key ingredients are made in Yorkshire and you can see who my suppliers are on page 196.

Undoubtedly, this is a fabulous pie and takes some making, but what a showstopper. The pie can be eaten anytime; you do not have to wait until Easter as it makes a great alternative to a Christmas stand pie.

For success, start this pie two days ahead of when you want to serve it if you can. The pastry needs a good rest, and the cooked pie must be completely cold before cutting; if it is too warm, it will collapse and is impossible to rescue.

serves 8

the pastry:
450 g plain flour, plus 3 tablespoons for rolling
250 g unsalted butter, cut roughly into ½ cm cubes
1 teaspoon Maldon salt
3 eggs

pie filling:
3 sweet, pointed red peppers
50 g baby spinach
2 tablespoons vegetable or other neutral oil
500 g Italian-style sausage
225 g ricotta cheese
4 eggs
4 tablespoons Parmesan, freshly grated
4 tablespoons pecorino, freshly grated
225 g mozzarella, 1 cm cubes
225 g smoked ham, 1 cm cubes
55 g Yorkshire salami slices
2 tablespoons flat-leaf parsley, finely chopped
25 g air-dried ham, finely sliced

Make the pastry

1.   Put the flour, butter, and salt into a food processor. Whizz until the mixture turns to a rough sand-like texture. Add the eggs and pulse 3 or 4 times until the pastry comes together. Tip onto the worktop and gently bring together into a ball. Wrap in clingfilm and put in the fridge to rest for at least half an hour.

2.   Lightly grease an 18 x 10 cm springform cake pan for a tall pie, or a 23 x 10 cm for one less tall but broader.

3.   Rolling the pastry to line whichever tin you choose is a little tricky, but this alternative way of doing it is surprisingly easy, and the results excellent. Reserve ¼ of the pastry for the lid, then tear the remainder into roughly 2.5 cm chunks, and first, press evenly onto the pan's base. Then continue up the sides in the same way to create the walls. Tear a large golf-ball-sized piece of dough, roll it into a ball, and press the base and sides of the pastry case to make an even thickness and smoothen out the pastry. Check it carefully to make sure there are no cracks or gaps. Finally, roll out a circle for the lid.

4.   Wrap your pastry case and lid loosely in clingfilm and put it into the fridge for several hours, preferably overnight if you can.

Prepare the pie filling:

1. Heat the oven to 200°C, lay the peppers on a baking tray, and roast in the oven until the skin is blackened, about 20 minutes. Wrap the peppers in clingfilm or slip them into a large plastic bag and tie tightly – be careful, they will be hot. Leave to go cold. Once cold, gently peel away the skin and wipe away any seeds.

2. Put the spinach into a large pan and put over medium heat, continually stirring until just wilted but not cooked. Remove the pan from the heat. Put a large colander into the sink, tip the spinach in, and using a wooden spoon or spatula, press firmly to squeeze out any excess water. Tip the drained spinach into a large bowl and, using a pair of kitchen scissors, chop roughly.

3. Heat the oil in a large frying pan. Squeeze the meat from the Italian sausage into the pan and fry for 6 minutes to cook through, continually stirring and breaking the meat into bite-sized chunks as you go. Tip the sausage onto a plate covered with kitchen paper and leave to go cold.

4. Place the ricotta into a roomy baking bowl. Add two of the eggs, half the 3 tablespoons of Parmesan and pecorino, the mozzarella, ham, salami, and parsley. Stir well to combine everything thoroughly.

5. Take the pie case from the fridge and lay the slices of air-dried ham over the base to make sure it is completely covered (this helps protect the base from going soggy).

6. Pour the ricotta mix and meat filling into the pastry case and tap the pan gently on the worktop to settle and level the mixture. Crumble the cooked sausage over, then cover with the strips of red pepper. Scatter over the remaining Parmesan and pecorino. Finally, sprinkle over the spinach for the final layer.

7. Beat the last egg in a small bowl. Wash the pie's rim and the lid with a little egg, then lay the lid on the pie, crimp to seal, and create a decorative edge. Cut a ½ cm hole in the centre of the lid and if you have any leftover pastry, decorate as you wish. Finally, egg-wash the top of the pie.

8. Place the hefty pie on a baking sheet and into the centre of the preheated oven. Bake for 70 minutes, until the pastry is golden brown, and the internal temperature has reached a minimum of 65°C.

9. Stand the pie on a cooling rack but do not even think about removing it from the tin for three to four hours; better still leave it longer if you can. Refrigerating overnight will firm up the pie beautifully and make it so easy to slice. This pie is best served cold and will keep well in the fridge for two or three days.

Ham Pot Pie

We love a pie in Yorkshire, and if Denby Dale pie is anything to go by, we like them big, as you can see on page 124. However, this lovely small pie has no aspirations; it is big enough in flavour.

The beauty of this pie is that it is a super way to use up leftover chunks of ham, maybe after Boxing Day or Easter. Use thick pieces of ham rather than slices, so you have decent-sized cubes, which is all the better for flavour.

serves 4

50 g carrots, peeled and cut into tiny cubes
4 tablespoons butter, plus extra for greasing
50 g onion, finely diced
40 g celery, thinly sliced
4 tablespoons plain flour
600 ml milk
pinch mace
pinch sea salt
freshly ground black pepper
1 egg, beaten
150 g of fresh vegetables (peas, beans and broccoli)
2 tablespoons parsley leaves, chopped
115 g leftover ham, cubed
320 g frozen puff pastry sheet, defrosted

1.   Grease either two 20 x 12 x 5 cm deep individual pie tins or a 20 x 5 cm deep pie plate. Put to one side.

2.   Bring 220 ml water to a boil in a small saucepan, add the diced carrots and cook for 3 minutes, strain and keep to one side.

3.   Melt the remaining butter in a large saucepan over medium heat, add the chopped onion and celery and gently fry for 5 minutes to soften but not brown.

4.   Sprinkle the flour onto the onion and celery, stir and cook for 2 minutes, then slowly add the milk a splash at a time stirring well between each addition. Next, add the mace, salt and pepper. Stir continuously until the sauce thickens to the consistency of double cream. Next, add half of the beaten egg and stir well.

5.   Finally, add the mixed vegetables to the sauce and stir; cook for 5 minutes. Remove from the heat and leave to cool down for 10–15 minutes. Once cooled, add the parsley and the ham.

6.   Heat oven to 200°C.

7. Lay the pastry on a lightly floured work surface and cut 2 pieces of pastry to line your tins, plus 2 for the lids. Or 2 circles to fit the pie plate. Line the base of your chosen tin. Fill with the ham and vegetable sauce.

8. Brush the pastry edges with a bit of cold water and lay the lid on. Press lightly, then crimp the edges with either your fingers or the edge of a fork to seal the pie.

9. Cut a hole the size of a pencil into the centre of each pie and brush it all over with the remaining beaten egg. Bake in the centre of the oven for 25–30 minutes until the pastry is golden and risen and the sauce is bubbling. Don't worry if it bubbles up through the hole, as this adds to the character of the pie.

10. Serve immediately with more fresh, seasonal vegetables of your choice.

Stromboli

It seems as if the whole world is in love with pizza and it's easy to understand why. It's tasty, filling, and home to so many toppings – there's always something for everyone. So, you'd think it would be hard to better the Italian classic; well, say hello to the stromboli, a dish that starts looking like a pizza but ends up more like a savoury roulade.

Traditionally, stromboli will have meats and mozzarella, but like its cousin, the pizza, almost anything you wish can go into the filling. Serve the stromboli hot from the oven, sliced up for a buffet table, eaten cold at a picnic – what more can you ask from one dish?

serves 6–8

the dough:
450 g plain flour
2 teaspoons (7 g) fast-acting dried yeast
1 teaspoon caster sugar
2 teaspoons salt
3 tablespoons extra virgin olive oil, plus extra to grease
220 ml lukewarm water
the filling:
350 ml tomato sauce (see page 183)
75 g chorizo sausage, chopped
75 g thick ham slices, chopped
1 x 125 g mozzarella ball, drained
50 g black olives, pitted
50 g fresh basil leaves

1. In a large bowl, mix the flour with the yeast, add the sugar and salt and mix again. Add the oil and water and mix to create a soft, slightly sticky dough. If the mixture feels dry, add a little more water, but more flour if too wet.

2. Turn the dough onto a floured surface and knead for at least 7 minutes to create a smooth and elastic dough. Coat a large baking bowl with oil, tip in the kneaded dough, cover with a tea towel and leave to rise in a warm, draft-free place until double the size; this will take at least an hour.

3. Cover a baking sheet with parchment paper and set aside.

4. Roll out the dough into a rectangle measuring approximately 45 x 35 cm. Slide this onto the baking sheet and reshape if it twists slightly.

5. Spread the tomato sauce over the dough, leaving a 1 cm margin around. Scatter the chorizo and ham evenly over the dough. Next, tear

the mozzarella ball into small chunks and scatter evenly over the meat followed by the black olives. Finally tear and scatter the basil over.

6. Lightly brush all 4 edges of the dough with plain water. Fold the short ends in about 1 cm. Then starting with the longest side close to you, loosely roll up the stromboli. Once rolled, tightly pinch the seam to seal in the filling and prevent it from springing open.

7. Cover the roll with lightly oiled clingfilm and leave it to rise in the same place as before for 30 minutes. Preheat the oven to 200°C.

8. Remove the clingfilm and lightly dust the stromboli with flour. Then, with a very sharp knife, make 6 to 8 slashes across the top to release the steam while cooking.

9. Bake in the centre of the hot oven for 30 minutes. The stromboli is ready when by gently rolling it on its side, checking the bottom is cooked and golden brown.

Dairy

There are some heavyweight cheesemakers in Yorkshire, not least the world-famous Wensleydale Creamery at Hawes. Cheese has been made in the dale for over 1000 years since French Cistercian monks settled there, but the first creamery only since 1897. The cheese is world renowned, helped partly by its association with Wallace and Gromit, but more because of the 20 handcrafted cheeses they produce.

Shepherds Purse near Thirsk is a much younger company with very well-regarded cheeses. I have known them since their beginning and had high regard for the late Judy Bell, who began making cheese with dairy alternatives for those with allergies to cows' milk. Their cheeses have won many awards, including the Super Gold at the World Cheese Awards in 2017.

Yorkshire is also stacked with artisan cheesemakers, as great as these larger companies are. It has some of the top cheesemongers in the country, not least Andy and Kathy Swinscoe at the Courtyard Dairy near Settle, though I also have a fondness for Love Cheese in York, where Harry Baines is making quite a name for himself too.

Over at the Courtyard, you can buy from an incredible range of cheeses from around the world, but it is the care they take to promote the smaller artisan cheesemakers which I find commendable, and a few can be found in the recipes here in this book. If you fancy a career change, Andy also runs cheesemaking courses for budding cheesemakers and those like me who just want to have a go.

But dairy is not just about cheese; there's butter, including my favourite goats' butter from St Helen's at Seaton Ross. There's cream, and Yorkshire is showing Cornwall a thing or two with the clotted cream from Sue Gaudie at Stamfrey Farm. Yoghurts are everywhere, including the famous Longley Farm and their award-winning range. But it is Hesper Skyr that has caught my attention and tastebuds; you can read about them on my ice lolly recipe.

And, of course, let's not forget the ice cream. We love our ice cream in Yorkshire, so it is no surprise there are far too many to mention here. There's Brymor and Yummy Yorkshire (their liquorice inspired the recipe on page 177), Mr Moo's and Yorvale, and on and on. Plus, for the number of ice cream makers, there are even more ice cream parlours across the county from the coast to the Dales, north and south. You won't have to go far to find one.

Finally, eggs. There are many great egg producers and I am pleased to say, many, though not all, are raising happy hens who are producing happy eggs. At Minskip near Boroughbridge we have the lovely Yolk Farm which is both a farm shop, egg restaurant, but primarily they have the happiest hens roaming around in the fresh air with access to the coop whenever they want. I love to go see them, knowing that they are living life as a hen should. As Farmer Ben and Emma will tell you, happy, healthy hens make healthier yummy eggs too and I agree.

Cheese and Onion Flan

Here in Yorkshire, we like a flan rather than a quiche, which sounds so much more homely and wholesome even though it is not too dissimilar to the ubiquitous French tart.

This delicious cheesy flan has lovely memories of my school dinners and was a favourite in the summer term served with new potatoes and salad and is one I continue to make as my family loves it too.

serves 6
1 quantity of shortcrust pastry (page 185)
for the filling:
55 g butter
2 tablespoons extra virgin olive oil or sunflower oil
1 large yellow onion, peeled and finely sliced
5 eggs
75 g mature Cheddar cheese, coarsely grated
2–3 tablespoons chopped flat-leaf parsley
200 ml milk
salt and freshly ground pepper

1. Make the pastry, then roll the pastry to 5 mm and line a greased, 25 cm loose-bottomed tart tin. Chill in the refrigerator while you continue making the filling.

2. Melt the butter and oil in a large frying pan over medium heat. Add the onion and cook slowly for 20 minutes until soft and golden but not browned. Remove from the heat and leave to cool.

3. Preheat the oven to 200°C.

4. Put the eggs into a large measuring jug. Add the cooled onions, the grated cheese, parsley, and top up with the milk until you have 700 ml, season with a good pinch of salt and pepper.

5. Take the pastry case from the refrigerator, place it on the middle shelf of the oven, carefully pour in the filling until it is two-thirds full. Do not overfill as the flan will rise in cooking. Bake for 30–40 minutes until the top is golden brown and set but not solid when gently pressed in the centre.

6. Remove from the oven and rest for 5 minutes before serving. The flan is lovely warm but can also be eaten at room temperature, but never straight from the fridge as this deadens the flavour.

Halloumi, Green Bean and Caper Salad

Salad on the plate in under 30 minutes is what we all desire on a warm summer's evening and one that is quick, easy, and nutritious, though this recipe translates beautifully to any time of year.

Here in Yorkshire, we have excellent halloumi made by the inspirational Syrian refugee Razan Alsous. With her husband and three children, she made the brave journey from war-torn Syria to settle in West Yorkshire. Having lost almost everything in the war and unable to find any great "squeaky cheese", as she calls halloumi, set about making it herself with the help of a £2500 start-up grant. That was back in 2014, and the cheese is now known all over the UK, not just in Yorkshire.

serves 2 as a main course, 4 as a starter

200 g new potatoes, sliced ½ cm thick
pinch of salt
200 g green beans, top and tailed
5 tablespoons extra virgin olive oil
1 tablespoon red wine vinegar
55 g baby capers, washed
2 tablespoons mint leaves, chopped
2 tablespoons dill leaves, chopped
100 g cherry tomatoes, halved
12 black olives, stoned
salt and pepper to taste
2 tablespoons plain flour
200 g halloumi cheese, sliced around 1 cm thick

1. Put the sliced potatoes into a large saucepan, cover with cold water and a pinch of salt. Bring to a rapid boil, lower the heat and simmer for 10–15 minutes or until the potatoes are cooked but not falling apart. Drain through a colander and keep to one side.

2. In another saucepan, bring another pan of salted water to a boil. Add the beans, cook for 2 minutes. Drain and keep to one side.

3. Mix 4 tablespoons of the oil and the vinegar in a medium-sized bowl, add the capers, mint and dill. Stir. Add the potatoes, beans, cherry tomatoes and olives. Stir to coat the vegetables and season with salt and pepper.

4. Heat the remaining tablespoon of oil to hot in a medium non-stick frying pan. Put the flour onto a plate and season the flour with salt and pepper. Dip the halloumi into the flour on both sides, tap to remove any surplus flour. Cook the halloumi on each side until golden brown.

5. Divide the salad between the plates with the halloumi slices on top. Serve immediately.

Lasagne di Bosco — Mushroom Lasagne

If you think the best lasagne involves a rich, meaty, tomato sauce, try this mushroom version and you may think again. This recipe was one of the most popular recipes at the cookery school in Tuscany. Though this recipe is without meat, for those who want or need some, we often layered in slices of salty Parma ham.

Use your favourite cultivated mushrooms and if you are lucky enough to be able to buy wild ones add them to the mix but no more than 50% as too many will overpower the dish.

serves 6

1 small carrot, finely chopped
½ small onion, finely chopped
½ stick celery, finely chopped
1 fresh bay leaf
500 ml milk, plus a little extra hot, if needed
55 g plain flour
55 g butter + 25 g for baking
sea salt and freshly ground pepper
10–15 dried lasagne sheets
450 g mixed mushrooms, wiped and thickly sliced
125 g Parmesan cheese, sliced very thinly + 25 g grated

1. Put all the vegetables into a large saucepan, add the bay leaf and milk then bring to a gentle simmer for 10 minutes. Do not boil the milk. Strain, discard the vegetables and keep the milk warm.

2. Melt the butter in a saucepan, add the flour and stir vigorously to make a thick paste. Slowly add the milk stirring continuously, lower the heat and stir until the sauce thickens. The sauce should have a thick pouring consistency, but if too thick, add a little hot milk.

3. Season with a little salt and pepper, stir for 1 minute then put to one side. Heat the oven to 190°C.

4. Rub a little butter onto the bottom and sides of a deep 23 cm x 23 cm ceramic lasagne dish. Put one ladleful of sauce on the bottom, spread around a little, and cover with lasagne sheets to fit the base. Cover the sheets with a generous layer of mushrooms, followed by Parmesan shavings, then sauce. Repeat to fill your dish or until all the ingredients are used up; always finish with a layer of sauce.

5. Sprinkle the grated cheese over and a small dusting of freshly ground pepper. Bake in the centre of the oven for around 30–40 minutes until the mushroom lasagne is bubbling and golden brown on the surface.

6. Remove from the oven and leave to stand for 10 minutes before serving. Enjoy with a green salad.

Quick Chickpea Curry

I have been making this super simple mild chickpea curry for years. I have no idea where the original recipe came from but thank you to wherever that was.

This curry is one of those dishes that comes together quickly and without fuss, making a super quick lunch or supper dish. Eat it with soft naan or roti.

serves 4

3 tablespoons vegetable oil
3 cloves garlic, peeled and finely chopped
4 cm piece of fresh ginger, peeled and finely chopped
2 teaspoons ground cumin
2 teaspoons ground coriander
200 g chopped tinned tomatoes, drained
150 ml vegetable stock
2 onions, peeled and chopped
225 g white mushrooms, sliced
1 x 425 g tin chickpeas, drained
3 tablespoons fresh coriander leaves, chopped
50 g creamed coconut
75 g toasted, flaked almonds
salt & pepper

1.   Heat 1 tablespoon of oil to hot but not smoking, and gently fry the garlic, ginger and spices for 2 to 3 minutes.

2.   Add the tomatoes and stock and cook for a further minute.

3.   Blend the ingredients in a liquidiser or food processor until smooth to create a curry paste.

4.   In the same pan, fry the onions in the remaining oil for 3 minutes, add the sliced mushrooms and cook for a further 3 minutes.

5.   Pour the curry paste over the onion and mushrooms, and add the drained chickpeas and two-thirds of the chopped coriander. Heat gently for 10 minutes.

6.   Stir in the creamed coconut and flaked almonds, reserving a few for garnish, and season to taste.

7.   Serve hot, garnished with the remaining coriander and a few toasted almonds.

Vegetarian Wellington

Whether you are a committed vegetarian or occasionally like to leave the meat alone, you are going to love this showstopper of a dish. The Wellington is usually associated with beef or game, but here, it is stacked with vegetables, mushrooms, good grains and bathed in a creamy tarragon sauce. The vegetarian Wellington does take some making but is so worth the effort.

serves 6

320 g ready-made puff pastry
100 g quick-cook farro
250 ml milk
15 g tarragon, finely chopped
175 g butternut squash, peeled, cut into 1 cm cubes
175 g sweet potato, peeled and cut into 1 cm cubes
5 tablespoons olive oil
sea salt and freshly ground black pepper
200 g large portobello mushrooms
50 g unsalted butter, plus a little for greasing
25 g baby kale or slice up regular kale but not too fine
1 tablespoon plain flour
1 medium free-range egg, lightly beaten
250 ml double cream

1.   Roll the pastry to create a rectangle 35 x 23 cm, cover with greaseproof paper and keep in the fridge until needed.

2.   Lightly grease a baking sheet and line with greaseproof paper. Put to one side.

3.   Add the farro to a small saucepan of lightly boiling water and cook for 10 minutes. Drain and spread on kitchen paper to drain.

4.   Heat the milk but do not boil. Add two-thirds of the tarragon leaves, stir, then put to one side to infuse. Heat the oven to 200°C.

5.   Tip the butternut squash and sweet potato cubes into a roasting tin. Sprinkle with the oil, a good pinch of sea salt and a few grinds of black pepper. Roll the vegetables around the tray to cover with oil and seasoning, then roast in the centre of the oven for 20 minutes. Once cooked, scoop onto kitchen paper to drain.

6.   Take the Portobello mushrooms, remove the stalk and keep to one side. Cut the mushroom into even 1 cm thick slices and keep any leftover bits and pieces with the stalk.

7.   In a large frying pan, heat half the butter until foaming, add the mushrooms and cook for 3 minutes, turning once, lift from the pan, and drain on kitchen paper. Keep the pan on the stove, add the kale and cook to wilt slightly then keep to one side.

8.   Melt the remaining butter in a saucepan, add the flour and stir quickly to form a thick paste. Strain the milk through a fine sieve into the pan and whisk like crazy until you have a glossy, smooth cream sauce – cook for a further 2 minutes.

9.   Finely chop the mushroom stalks along with any leftover mushroom bits, add to the cream sauce, stir, and add the farro and stir again. Season with a small pinch of salt and pepper. Keep to one side to cool.

10.   Cut the pastry sheet into 2 equal pieces 17.5 x 23 cm and put one onto the prepared baking tray.

assemble the Wellington:

11.   With the narrow end of the pastry in front of you, cover with the baby kale leaving a 2.5 cm margin all the way around.

12.   Spoon over a thick layer of the farro cream, tuck buttery slices of mushrooms into the sauce starting from front to back and don't worry if there are gaps.

13.   Then, carefully tuck the squash and potatoes on and around the mushroom, filling any gaps and finishing with more farro piled on top.

14.   Brush around pastry lightly with beaten egg and lay the second sheet of pastry over carefully, stretching it to fit like a pie. Then, gently mould the pastry into a log shape using your hands.

15.   Firmly press the edges together to seal while keeping the 2.5 cm margin, then use the back of a fork to press the edges to create an even firmer seal. Finally, neaten the edges and use any bits of pastry to decorate.

16.   Brush the top and sides of the Wellington with beaten egg and, using a sharp knife, score the pastry 4 or 5 times, taking care not to cut right through.

17.   Put the Wellington, uncovered, into the fridge to chill and rest for at least 2 hours.

18.   Heat the oven to 200°C. Cook the Wellington in the centre of the oven for 40 minutes until golden brown and well risen. Leave to rest for 10 minutes.

19.   Heat the double cream with the remaining tarragon and simmer gently until reduced by a third, stirring from time to time. Once cooked, keep to one side until needed.

20.   To serve the Wellington, cut into thick slices and serve with the tarragon cream sauce in a jug on the side.

Kitchen notes: you can make the Wellington the day before up to step 17, wrap in greaseproof paper and keep it in the fridge. Take it from the fridge about 30 minutes before cooking it.

Torta di Pomodoro – Tomato Tart

If I had to choose one tart and declare it my all-time favourite, it would be this one from the school in Tuscany which uses my ubiquitous sauce. Why is this my favourite? Simply because it is delicious.

serves 4–6

1 quantity of pastry (page 185)
3 large eggs, lightly beaten
50 g freshly grated Parmesan
1 quantity of cold rich tomato sauce (page 183)

1. Make the pastry then butter a 25 cm loose-bottomed tart tin. Roll the pastry to 5 mm thick and line the tin. Pop it into the fridge.

2. Add the eggs and Parmesan to the tomato sauce and mix very well with a wooden spoon in a large baking bowl. Heat the oven to 200°C.

3. Place the pastry case on the middle shelf of the oven, carefully pour in the filling until it is two-thirds full. Do not overfill as the flan will rise in cooking. Bake for 30 minutes or until the top starts to brown and is set but not solid when gently pressed in the centre.

4. Remove the tart from the oven and rest for 15 minutes before serving. The tart is lovely warm but can also be eaten at room temperature, but never straight from the fridge as this deadens the flavour. Serve with a rocket or other green salad.

Farro Risotto

Farro is one of those wonderful grains that you will return to time and time again because it is so easy to cook and delivers a whole bunch of nutritional goodness on your plate. In addition, farro is classed as an ancient grain because it has been around for centuries and has seen a significant resurgence in recent times.

I first had this grain while working in Tuscany where it is hugely popular and loved that, although not rice, it does make a fabulous risotto-style dish without all the hassle and standing over the stove stirring. It also keeps a bite, like risotto rice, but with a nuttier, heavier taste.

serves 4

25 g wild mushrooms, dried
800 ml water
160 g farro
4 teaspoons clarified butter or ghee
1 shallot, finely chopped
1 large clove garlic, finely chopped
2 tablespoons parsley leaves, finely chopped
50 g freshly grated Parmesan

1.   Place the mushrooms into a heatproof bowl and cover with boiling water. Leave to one side for 30 minutes while the mushrooms rehydrate.

2.   Bring 800 ml of water to a boil in a large stockpot. Add the farro, cover, and simmer for 15 minutes. Once cooked, drain through a colander and keep to one side.

3.   Heat the clarified butter or ghee in a large frying pan. Add the chopped shallot and cook for 10 minutes on medium heat keeping an eye on the shallot to make sure it does not burn.

4.   Lower the heat and add the garlic, cook for 5 minutes.

5.   Drain the dried mushrooms through a fine sieve set over a bowl, keeping the mushroom water.

6.   Finely chop the mushrooms and add to the pan with the shallot and garlic. Cook for 5 minutes. Add the drained farro to the frying pan and stir.

7.   Add 4 tablespoons of the mushroom water and raise the heat, cook until all the water has evaporated. Add the parsley and stir again. Cook for 5 minutes more.

8.   Serve the farro risotto in warmed bowls with a generous handful of freshly grated Parmesan.

Simple Pumpkin Risotto

There is something so wonderful about a simple, unfussy risotto made without too much fuss and too many additional ingredients; let the creamy rice and cheese do their thing, I say. Here I have added a little pumpkin which works so well in a risotto, adding some texture and a sweet flavour. You can, of course, add other ingredients; a little freshly chopped parsley at the end works well.

How much Parmesan is a matter of choice. My preference is to grate it over the cooked rice as in this recipe and taste until you get that hit of cheese rather than overpowering it.

Another ingredient you will need, aside from those listed, is time. You cannot and must not rush making this dish. Instead, turn off your phone, turn up some gentle music and enjoy stirring in the stock and watching the dish come alive.

50 g salted butter + 1 tablespoon
1 small onion, finely chopped
1 clove of garlic, crushed
125 ml of good white wine
250 g arborio rice
750 ml vegetable stock or water
250 g pumpkin cut into small cubes
tiny pinch of nutmeg, grated
salt and pepper
freshly grated Parmesan, as required
chopped flat-leaf parsley, optional

1. Melt the 50 g of butter in a wide heavy-based pan, add the onion and garlic, and slowly cook until the onion is softened. Turn the heat up a little, add the wine, and let it bubble for a few minutes.

2. Add the rice, and when thoroughly coated in butter, add the hot stock a ladleful at a time until two-thirds of the stock is absorbed. Do not rush this part; gently stirring and allowing the rice to soften creates a creamy 'al-dente' rather than rice pudding texture.

3. Add the pumpkin, and stir through the risotto. Add a couple more ladlefuls of stock and let the pumpkin bubble gently in the rice until tender but not falling apart. Add the remaining stock, again a little at a time, until the risotto is thick and creamy.

4. Add the nutmeg and a generous grating of Parmesan to your taste (you also put more cheese on the table for those who may want more). Serve on warmed plates with parsley sprinkled over if you wish.

Apple, Blackberry and Walnut Crumble Cake

serves 6

for the crumble:
45 g self-raising flour
3 tablespoons jumbo rolled oats
35 g caster sugar
1 teaspoon ground cinnamon
½ teaspoon ground mace
sea salt
40 g unsalted butter, chilled and
    finely diced
25 g walnuts, roughly chopped

for the cake:
3 crisp apples (Cox, Braeburn, Granny
    Smith)
juice ½ lemon
250 g unsalted butter, softened, plus
    extra for greasing
225 g golden caster sugar
4 large free-range eggs
125 g ground almonds
180 g self-raising flour
1 teaspoon ground cinnamon
1 teaspoon baking powder
125 g fresh blackberries

1. Heat the oven to160°C. Grease a 24 x 4 cm deep square cake tin with butter and line with baking parchment.

2. Stir the flour, oats, sugar, cinnamon, mace and a pinch of sea salt together.

3. Add the butter and rub together to create buttery rubble-like chunks. Add the walnuts and mix in carefully. Tip into a plastic bag, put into the freezer for 30 minutes until frozen.

4. Quarter and core each apple, cut into three thick slices, toss in the lemon juice, and put to one side.

5. In a large baking bowl, using an electric hand or stand mixer, cream the butter and sugar until light and pale; or use a fork, but it takes longer. Whisk in the eggs one at a time; if the mixture starts to curdle, add a tablespoon of the flour to bring it back together.

6. In another bowl, mix the almonds, flour, cinnamon, and baking powder. Using a large spoon or spatula, carefully cut and fold into the butter, sugar and egg mixture. Be gentle, you do not want to lose the air in the cake batter.

7. Place half the mixture into the prepared tin, gently level the mix with the back of a spoon, then lay slices of apple on the surface and gently press down a little. Repeat with the remaining mix and apple slices. Finish by pressing the blackberries into the surface.

8. Remove the crumble from the freezer, bash it gently with a rolling pin to break it up slightly. Sprinkle over the cake and bake for 50 minutes in the centre of the oven or until golden brown: it is ready when a skewer inserted into the middle comes out clean.

9. Remove from the oven and cool in the tin for half an hour. Then, transfer to a wire rack. Once cooled, serve with vanilla ice cream or custard.

Old-Fashioned Apple Charlotte

The Charlotte is a traditional English pudding that seems to have fallen off the radar in recent years which is hard to understand as it really is a lovely pudding. What's not to like about bread a few days old slathered in melted butter, filled with stewed apples, then baked.

serves 6

450 g crisp green apples, peeled and sliced
2 tablespoons butter plus 110 g butter, melted
2 tablespoons dark brown sugar
6 slices thick white farmhouse-style bread, 2 or 3 days old

1. Peel, core, and roughly chop the apples into equal chunks. Melt the 2 tablespoons of butter with the brown sugar on medium heat in a saucepan large enough to hold the apples. Add the apple pieces, stir, then cook gently for 10 minutes until the apples are starting to soften. Remove from the heat and keep to one side.

2. Generously brush the bottom and sides of a 15 cm pudding basin with a little melted butter. Take one slice of the bread, remove the crusts, and cut to fit the base. Brush butter over both sides of the bread disc and then fit snugly into the base.

3. Remove the crusts from your remaining slices of bread, keep one slice to one side for the lid and cut the remaining into rectangles approximately 8 x 4 cm. You will need enough rectangles to line the sides of the pudding basin with a slight overlap and reaching to the upper rim of the bowl. Paint the bread generously with butter; the bread should be saturated. Fill the bowl with the cooked apples.

4. Cut the last slice of bread into a circle and lay on the top, butter well. Preheat the oven to 180°C.

5. Cut a circle of thick cardboard to fit inside the rim of the bowl. Cover this with foil and lay it on top of the Charlotte and press it down slightly. This is to help make an even base when the Charlotte is unmoulded.

6. Place the dish on a baking sheet and cook in the centre of the preheated oven for 30 minutes until the bread is golden down the sides. You can see this by gently lifting the cardboard lid and seeing if the edges are turning golden brown. Once this happens, remove the cardboard lid and cook for 8 minutes longer to brown the top. It will not go as golden as the sides but don't worry; this will be the base when cooked.

7. Remove from the oven and cover with a plate. Flip over and the Charlotte should drop neatly onto the plate. Serve at once with custard or whipped cream.

Brioche and Cranberry Bread and Butter Pudding

This is a slightly posh version of a traditional bread and butter pudding and is a great way to use leftover brioche rolls, or any bread for that matter (if slices of bread, then cut into triangles instead).

serves 4

55 g butter, at room temperature
6 soft brioche rolls, cut into 3 diagonally
55 g dried cranberries
2 tablespoons port
350 ml full-fat milk
50 ml double cream
2 large eggs
4 tablespoons caster sugar
1 teaspoon vanilla extract

1. Preheat the oven to 180°C. Grease a 1½ litre ovenproof rectangular baking dish with a bit of butter.

2. Spread one side of each slice of brioche with the remaining butter.

3. Arrange the brioche slices slightly overlapping, butter-side up on the base of the dish

4. Sprinkle half the cranberries evenly over the bread, then lightly sprinkle with 1 tablespoon of the port. Repeat one more time or until the dish is filled, finishing with the cranberries on top.

5. Gently heat the milk and cream in a saucepan but do not boil. Set aside.

6. In a medium-sized heatproof bowl, beat the eggs with 3 tablespoons of the sugar and the vanilla extract until light, airy, and pale in colour.

7. Slowly pour the warm (not hot) milk over the eggs, whisking continuously until all the milk is added.

8. Pour the egg mixture slowly and evenly over the bread until all the liquid is added. Gently press the bread down into the liquid. Sprinkle the remaining tablespoon of sugar over the surface and set aside for 30 minutes.

9. Bake the pudding in the hot oven for 40–45 minutes, or until the surface is golden brown, the pudding is well risen, and the eggs are set. Serve hot and enjoy.

Sweet Tooth Yorkshire

Without a doubt, we have a sweet tooth here in Yorkshire, which could be one of the reasons the county was and still is home to more confectionery companies than anywhere else in Britain. The history and heritage of the craft of sweet-making encompass more than the Yorkshire desire for 'sommat' sweet and it is not a pure coincidence either that confectionery landed here, though we are all, of course, grateful that it did.

So Why Yorkshire?

Various factors gave rise to sweet-making with one major factor being the excellent transport links both in and out of the county. Yorkshire was central to the trading routes from the south through to Scotland with York ideally placed en-route. The city had quickly embraced the fashion for chocolate houses, already famous in London from the mid-17th century and deemed as the forerunners of the pub. York quickly became both a very sociable and fashionable stopping-off place.

But, by far the most significant influence was the easy access along the Ouse from the east coast ports where shipments of both cocoa beans, sugar and fruits arrived from the near continent where sweet-making, especially chocolate confectionery, had taken hold long before it did in Britain.

Thus the raw materials needed came in and, once made, the ever popular rail links to major cities including London took the sweets and chocolates outwards and onwards and their popularity soared.

York has possibly played the largest part in the sweetie heritage of Yorkshire with much of the credit given to the abstemious Quaker movement that had a stronghold in the city. The benign nature of cocoa was not lost on them and, from humble beginnings, the three top players of the 18th century in chocolate and other confectionery were Rowntree's, Terry's and Craven – of the toffees and humbugs fame.

The former two went on to become global brands and at one time employed more than 14,000 people in the chocolate industry in the city. The philanthropic benevolence born of their Quaker origins saw workers given paid holidays, company pensions, doctors and dentists and many of the good works continue today in the charitable works seen at New Earswick Village and the Joseph Rowntree Foundation.

More Sweets in Yorkshire

It is not merely the leading world brands like Rowntree's, Terry's and Mackintosh who are synonymous with confectionery in the county. There are many other companies that, though smaller, have a big place in the hearts and memories of sweet-lovers far and wide. As Paul Chrystal mentions in his fascinating book, *Confectionery in Yorkshire Through Time* covering both the industrial and social and economic history of sweets here, some of these companies still exist today; others are long gone or have been taken over by more major players; names such as Thornton's, Needlers of Hull, Dobsons of Elland, and Lion's of Cleckheaton which is still a thriving brand today. It would be remiss not to add to the list the likes of Dunhill Aniseed Balls and Wilkinsons Pontefract Cakes, Farrah's Toffee, Nuttall's Mintoes from Doncaster, and Slade and Bullock in Dewsbury who made the first lettered rock. What would the seaside be without it today?

Chocolate and Confectionery in Yorkshire Today

As with many artisan and heritage foods, chocolate and confectionery are enjoying a renaissance with a wealth of small producers once more creating exciting, high quality, handmade products. York enjoys a highly successful chocolate festival each year and interest in learning chocolate and confectionery crafts is evident with the number of courses on offer in cookery schools and at venues, such as the city's first dedicated chocolate house since the 1820s, the Cocoa House in York.

Thanks to this demand for a true, artisan product, these are once more exciting times for chocolatiers and confectioners in York and throughout Yorkshire.

Gluten-Free Chocolate and Amaretto Torte

This is not just an utterly delicious chocolate tart laced with luscious almond flavour from the amaretto, it is also gluten-free so a super recipe for anyone for whom this is a problem (or not).

serves 6

250 g butter plus 1 tablespoon for greasing
250 g milk chocolate, coarsely chopped
8 large eggs, separated
125 g soft dark brown sugar
200 g caster sugar
4 tablespoons amaretto
65 g cocoa powder plus extra for dusting
125 g raspberries (optional)

1. Preheat the oven to 160°C.

2. Lightly grease a 23 cm springform tin and line the base and sides with greaseproof paper and put to one side.

3. In a non-stick saucepan gently melt the remaining butter on a low heat. Add the chocolate pieces to the pan and stir until melted. Remove from the heat as soon as melted and leave to cool for 10 minutes, but no longer or it will be too thick to stir in the remaining ingredients.

4. Beat the egg yolks with both sugars and amaretto using a stand mixer or hand whisk. Sift the cocoa powder through a fine sieve over the egg and sugar mixture, then on a very low speed – you do not want to beat the air out or the cake will not rise – gently mix.

5. Put the egg whites in a clean bowl and whisk until the whites start to stiffen and start to turn glossy.

6. The chocolate should now be cooled, so gently fold this into the egg mixture with a metal tablespoon. Then, stir in one-third of the beaten egg whites to loosen it, and then fold in the rest of the egg whites making sure the batter is evenly coloured with no chocolate streaks.

7. Carefully spoon the mixture into the prepared tin. Before baking, tap the tin on the work surface a few times to release any trapped air bubbles.

8. Bake in the centre of the oven for 50 minutes, or until set with the centre springing lightly. If the surface of the cake cracks, do not worry, consider it a feature of this cake. Remove from the oven and

place the pan on a cooling rack and leave to cool completely.

9. Before serving, heavily drench the cake with a dusting of cocoa powder and decorate. Raspberries work very well with this tart, and I recommend the simple sauce below and a few berries on top for a stunning finish.

Raspberry sauce: to make a simple raspberry sauce put 100 g raspberries into a blender or food processor and blitz. Push the sauce through a fine sieve to remove any seeds and drizzle on or around the cake. Decorate with the remaining berries and perhaps a little fresh mint.

If not eating at once, store the undecorated cake in an airtight container. The cake will keep for 2 to 3 days in a cool place but not in the refrigerator. Decorate before serving.

My Easy Chocolate Brownies

Tall, fudgy, and oh so delicious nut brownies. Easy to make and even easier to eat as they are so moreish.

makes 6–8 depending on the size

250 g unsweetened chocolate
225 g butter
300 g walnuts or pecan, chopped
5 eggs
500 g golden caster sugar
1 tablespoon vanilla extract
180 g plain flour

1. Generously butter a 20 x 23 cm baking tin and preheat the oven to 160°C.

2. Melt the chocolate and butter in a medium-sized bowl over a pan of lightly simmering water, making sure the bowl does not touch the water. Stir with a silicone spatula or wooden spoon. Once combined, remove from the heat and set aside to slightly cool.

3. Line a baking sheet with foil and sprinkle with the nuts, and roast in the centre of the oven for 15 minutes or until toasty brown but not burnt.

4. Cream the eggs, sugar and vanilla together in a large mixing bowl for 10 minutes, or if you have one, in a stand mixer, which will make it much easier. Then, beat in the flour.

5. Still stirring, slowly add the cooled chocolate. Finally, mix the nuts in by hand.

6. Pour the mixture into the tin and level carefully using a spatula or the back of a tablespoon. Bake for 35–40 minutes, keeping a close eye on it to avoid overbaking; the brownies should be rich, chocolatey and gooey.

7. Put the brownies onto a cooling rack to cool down then cut them to the size you want. Store the brownies in an airtight box or tin; they are best eaten sooner rather than later but will keep for a few days.

Super-Rich Gluten-Free Chocolate Flan

Do not be deceived by the shallow depth of this chocolate flan – what it lacks in size, it makes up for with sheer richness and decadent cocoa flavour, and as there is no flour, the flan is also gluten-free.

With no flour to stabilise the flan, it is delicate to both make and cook. But, using a water bath – aka bain-marie – helps carefully set the eggs and chocolate into a light, melting texture by not cooking too quickly and helps keep it from drying out.

The chocolate flan looks lovely as is, or finish it with a bit of fresh fruit, a drizzle of caramel sauce, or chocolate shavings.

serves 8

55 g 50–60% dark chocolate
225 g plus 2 tablespoons butter, softened
6 eggs
150 g caster sugar

1. Preheat the oven to 120°C.

2. Grease a 23 x 8 cm springform cake tin and line the bottom with greaseproof paper. Wrap a band of clingfilm around the bottom and up the sides of the pan to keep any water from leaking into the flan while cooking in the water bath.

3. Melt the chocolate by breaking it into small pieces in a metal bowl over a pan of lightly simmering water (the bottom of the bowl should not touch the water).

4. Chop the 225 g of softened butter into small pieces and add to the bowl. Let these two gently melt together and only stir when melted using a wooden spoon or silicone spatula. Once melted, remove from the heat and let it stand for 2 minutes.

5. Put the eggs and sugar into a stand mixer and whisk on high speed until the mixture has quadrupled and turned a pale yellow; this will take around 10 minutes.

6. Slowly add the melted chocolate into the eggs and sugar with the mixer on low speed. Raise the speed a little and whisk until all the chocolate is combined. Note that the volume you created in the eggs will drop substantially with the addition of the chocolate.

7. Place the prepared cake tin into a large roasting dish. Pour the chocolate batter carefully into the tin. Lift the roasting tin a few inches, then tap it onto the worktop several times to release any air bubbles. Put the tin back into the oven and pour boiling water to fill.

8. Bake for 1½ hours, then check to see if the flan is cooked by gently shaking the pan. If cooked, the flan will be firm and not wobble. If it wobbles, cook another 15 minutes and check again.

9. Place the tin onto a cooling rack and leave the flan to cool in the tin. Once completely cool, chill in the fridge uncovered for at least 4 hours.

10. When ready to eat, run a knife around the edge and remove the sides of the springform. If any tiny bits stick, just use a warm palette knife to smooth the cake so it is smooth and shiny. Decorate as you wish. The cake will keep for a few days in an airtight tin, preferably in the fridge

Chocolate Swirl Cheesecake

This no-bake cheesecake is a real favourite, it takes no time to make and always receives heaps of praise. Here, it is made with dark chocolate but there is no reason to not switch this to milk if you prefer.

serves 6

for the crust:	for the filling:	for the chocolate swirl:
300 g chocolate biscuits	295 ml double cream	175 g dark chocolate,
115 g butter, melted	350 g full-fat cream cheese	broken into pieces

make the crust:

1. Grease a 20 cm loose-bottom cake tin, line the bottom with greaseproof paper and put it to one side.

2. Quickly blitz the chocolate biscuits in a food processor until they resemble coarse sand. Be careful not to over mix, or the base will be hard.

3. No food processor? Simply put the biscuits into a plastic bag and crush lightly with a rolling pin.

4. Pour the butter over the crumbs, stir well to ensure they are all covered.

5. Spoon the crumbs into the cake tin base, spreading them evenly and making sure there are no holes or cracks. Using a glass with a smooth flat bottom, level the crust by pressing the crumbs with the glass. Pop the base into the fridge for around an hour.

Make the cheesecake

6. Whip up the cream to firm but still soft peaks. Be careful not to overwhip, or the cream will start to curdle.

7. Carefully fold in the cream cheese until a smooth, glossy cream forms.

8. Take the base out of the fridge and gently spoon the filling onto the crust making sure there are no gaps. Level the cheesecake using the back of a tablespoon or palette knife and return it to the fridge.

Decorate the cheesecake

9. Put the chocolate pieces into a heatproof bowl and set over a pan of lightly boiling water, making sure the bottom of the bowl is not touching the water. Stir with a wooden spoon when melted.

10. Working quickly and using a teaspoon, drop small dots of chocolate over the surface of the cheesecake. Do not linger at this point, as the chocolate will start to set.

11. Using a metal skewer, quickly swirl the chocolate blobs through the filling. Don't be too precious here; the marbling should be random, both thick and thin, to resemble the marks on a marble slab.

12. Return the cheesecake to the fridge and chill until needed.

Summer Berry Galette

Quick, easy and bursting with fruit wrapped in a sweet, crumbly pastry is just about as easy as it comes to a summer dessert.

serves 6

175 g plain flour
85 g butter, cubed
55 g caster sugar
1 egg, beaten
splash of milk
400 g fresh summer
    berries
6 tablespoons of cold
    water
2 tablespoons
    cornflour
caster sugar for
    sprinkling

1. Sieve the flour into a bowl, add the butter and one-third of the sugar and rub the butter into the flour with your fingertips as quickly as possible until the mixture is like fine sand. Add the egg and mix to create a soft dough; if the mixture is too dry, add the splash of milk. Wrap the pastry in clingfilm and leave it to rest in the fridge for 30 minutes.

2. While the pastry is resting, put the berries into a saucepan with the remaining sugar. Add 4 tablespoons of cold water and bring to a very gentle simmer, do not stir, just shake the pan gently. You do not want to cook the berries, just heat them until they release a little juice.

3. Mix the cornflour with 2 tablespoons of cold water and add to the saucepan and cook until the sauce thickens; at this point, you can stir gently. Put to one side to cool.

4. Preheat the oven to 200°C.

5. Take the pastry from the fridge and roll it between two sheets of parchment paper to create a 25 cm circle. Remove the top sheet of parchment but leave the bottom one in place and slide the pastry circle and paper onto a baking sheet.

6. Pour the cold berry sauce into the centre of the dough and ever so carefully flip over the edges of the crust to hold the berries in.

7. Sprinkle the pastry and berries with caster sugar. Bake in the hot oven for 20–30 minutes until the crust is golden brown and the berries are lightly bubbling.

8. Serve hot or cold with freshly whipped cream or ice cream.

Zingy Tuscan Lemon Tart

A lemon tart truly is one of life's pleasures, from the tanginess of the lemon, to the creamy and buttery filling inside sweet, crumbling pastry. The French have their tarte au citron; we have our lemon meringue, and the Tuscans, this torta al limone.

I started making this tart at the school in Italy, and it was hugely popular to both make in class and eat at dinner. I prefer the filling here to the British version using cornflour. This Tuscan tart is more set and richer, which is no surprise given the number of eggs and amount of butter.

serves 8
1 quantity of pastry (page 185)
for the filling:
7 lemons, grated zest and
    juiced
350 g caster sugar
6 whole eggs
9 egg yolks
300 g unsalted butter, softened

1. Butter a 25 cm loose-bottomed tart tin, then make the pastry and roll to 5 mm on a floured work surface. Line the tart dish making sure there are no holes. Prick the base of the dish using a fork. Refrigerate for 15 minutes. Heat the oven to 190°C then blind bake as instructions on page 187.

2. For the filling, place the lemon zest, juice, sugar, eggs and egg yolks into a large roomy saucepan. Over very low heat, whisk to incorporate all the ingredients and continue whisking until the sugar has dissolved.

3. Add half of the softened butter and whisk again. Take your time with this process, do not be tempted to turn the heat up, or you will scramble the eggs. Slowly, the mixture will begin to thicken, and as it does, add the remaining softened butter and whisk well. The filling is ready when thick enough to coat the back of a wooden spoon.

4. Remove the pan from the heat and place it on a cold surface. Continue to whisk for 5 minutes to cool the mixture down.

5. Raise the oven temperature to 230°C. Pour the mixture into the pastry base, place near the top of the hot oven and bake until the top is brown, about 8 minutes.

6. Remove from the oven onto a cooling rack and leave the tart in the tin to cool completely. Serve only at room temperature, never hot and never straight from the fridge, which can deaden the flavour of the tart.

Lemon Ricotta Pancakes

You do not have to, but I suggest you may want to make these fluffy pancakes with yet another fantastic Yorkshire product, ricotta (others will work, but this is the best for me). One small-scale artisan cheesemaker, Yorkshire Pecorino, produces the award-winning Italian cheese surprisingly in Leeds. This was the first cheese from Italian-born Mario Olianas, but his range now includes a Leeds Blue, a grilling pecorino, and ricotta so fresh and creamy you will never again buy the mass-produced cheese.

makes 12 depending on size

3 eggs
175 g Yorkshire ricotta
75 ml cup whole milk
1 lemon, zest plus 2 tablespoons juice
85 g plain flour
1 teaspoon baking powder
½ teaspoon salt
2 tablespoons butter

1. Separate the eggs, in a large bowl add the yolks to the ricotta and the milk and whisk together to form a thick batter.

2. Using a stand, or electric hand mixer, whisk the egg whites until foamy, add one teaspoon of the lemon juice and continue to whisk until you have firm peaks.

3. Sieve the flour and baking powder into a large baking bowl, add the salt, then gradually beat in the batter, and keep whisking until thick and smooth. Finally, add the lemon zest and remaining juice.

4. Take 2 or 3 tablespoons of the beaten egg whites and whisk into the batter to loosen it. Then, carefully fold in the remaining egg whites while taking care not to lose too much air.

5. Heat a griddle, crêpe pan, or small frying pan to medium-hot and smear with a tiny piece of butter. Drop tablespoon dollops of batter onto the pan. Cook for 1–2 minutes until bubbles rise to the surface. Flip the pancake over and cook on the other side. Keep them warm while you continue cooking more until you have used up all the batter.

6. Lemon and ricotta pancakes are best eaten at once. For me, they are lovely with a smearing of butter on top, maybe a drizzle of honey or even an extra squeeze of lemon.

Lavender Cup Cakes

I wanted to include these tasty buns in the book in honour of the fabulous lavender grown here in Yorkshire, at – surprise, surprise – Yorkshire Lavender just outside Terrington in North Yorkshire; a place I always think of as our little bit of Provence here in the north of England. And well worth a visit if you are in the area.

makes 12

for the cake:
175 g butter, cut into small pieces
175 g self-raising flour
175 g caster sugar
pinch baking powder
3 eggs
½ teaspoon vanilla extract
2 teaspoons culinary lavender, plus
    extra for decoration

for the buttercream:
175 g butter
½ teaspoon vanilla extract
3 tablespoons milk
350 g icing sugar
lavender-coloured gel food
    colouring
culinary lavender for decoration

1. Preheat the oven to 175°C and put 12 paper cupcake cases into a 12-hole muffin tin.

2. Put all the cake ingredients into either a mixer or baking bowl and beat everything together to create a lovely smooth cake batter.

3. As carefully as you can, divide the mixture between cases and, using the back of a teaspoon, ever so gently smooth the surface of the mix.

4. Pop the cakes onto the middle shelf of the oven and bake for 20 minutes until risen and are golden brown. Remove from the oven and leave to cool for 5 minutes in the tin, then remove and leave to cool completely on a wire cooling rack.

5. Put the butter, vanilla, and 2 tablespoons milk into a large bowl, sift in half the icing sugar and a few drops of lavender food colouring. Beat fiercely with a wooden spoon to create a light, airy cream. Continue beating as you add the remaining sugar and a little milk if the mixture feels too dry.

6. Once the cupcakes are cold, it is time to be artistic. Pipe the buttercream onto the cakes in swirls, twists, ribbons, or whatever you like. Finish with a sprinkling of lavender. The cakes will only keep for a day or so, even in an airtight tin, so they are best eaten as soon as possible.

Red Velvet Trifle

Red velvet is hardly classic Yorkshire, far from it, but trifle is. I like a bit of dense, moist red velvet cake. It works well in a trifle and doesn't go as soggy as regular sponge cake or fingers usually do.

serves 6

115 g butter, softened plus extra for greasing
100 g caster sugar
1 teaspoon vanilla extract
1 medium free-range egg
120 ml buttermilk, sour cream or kefir
50 g dark cocoa powder
125 g plain flour
½ teaspoon baking powder
1 teaspoon bicarbonate of soda
½ teaspoon red food gel
450 g red and blue summer berries mixed, fresh or frozen
250 ml ready-made custard
250 ml double cream, lightly whipped

1. Preheat the oven to 180°C. Line a large baking sheet with baking paper.

2. Put the butter, sugar, and vanilla into the stand mixer bowl or use an electric hand mixer or a wire whisk. Beat for at least 5 minutes until the mixture is pale in colour and light and fluffy in texture. Add the egg and beat again; finally, add the buttermilk and mix thoroughly.

3. Sieve the cocoa powder, flour, baking powder, and bicarbonate of soda together, then gently beat into the butter mix. Finally, add the red food gel to get the colour you want, making sure to add the tiniest drop at a time as the gel is intense.

4. Spread the cake mixture into a 23 – 25 cm diameter circle on the baking sheet using a palette knife to ensure the batter is evenly spread. Cook the cake in the centre of the preheated oven for 10–12 minutes; the cake is ready when it is slightly firm to the touch in the centre. Remove and leave to cool on the tray for 5 minutes, then onto a cooling rack and leave to go cold.

5. Choose either individual glasses, or one large dish. Once the cake is cold, using a sharp knife, cut the cake into circles to fit your chosen glass or dish. Aim for at least 2 slices for each. Keep the leftover crumbs to use for decoration.

6. Place one slice of cake on the base and cover with a generous layer of mixed berries followed by a layer of thick custard, then another layer of cake followed by berries again. Finish with a layer of whipped cream and garnish with fruits and cake crumbs. Serve at once.

Homemade Gelato

There's no need to wait for your next trip to Italy to enjoy gelato at home as it is really easy to make with or without an ice cream machine, and instructions for both methods are included in this recipe.

Gelato has more milk in it than cream, so less fat, which means it freezes at a lower temperature, so is arguably easier to make without a machine.

Makes about 1 litre

568 ml whole milk
3 teaspoons vanilla extract
85 g caster sugar
55 g skimmed milk powder
4 large egg yolks

1. Put the milk, 1 teaspoon of vanilla extract, 2 teaspoons of the sugar and the milk powder into a large saucepan and stir well. Simmer on medium heat for 5 minutes, then remove from the heat and leave to infuse while preparing the other ingredients.

2. Place the egg yolks into a stand mixer with the remaining vanilla extract and sugar and whisk until the eggs are light and fluffy, around 10 minutes. Put a mixing bowl large enough to hold the custard into the freezer, or chill right down by filling with ice cubes.

3. Gently reheat the milk to warm but not hot or you risk it curdling. With the mixer running on medium speed, slowly and gently pour the liquid over the beaten eggs; take your time, do not rush this process.

4. Return the mixture back to the milk pan, place over low heat and, stirring continuously, cook gently until the mixture thickens enough to coat the back of a metal spoon.

5. Pour the mixture into the chilled-down bowl and continue to stir until cold enough to put back into the fridge. Cut a circle of greaseproof paper and lay this on the surface to prevent a skin forming and put it into the fridge for 3 to 4 hours or even overnight. Then, churn in your ice cream machine following the manufacturer's instructions.

Without an Ice Cream Machine

6. Put the cooled custard into the freezer for 30 minutes. Take it out and beat with either a fork, hand whisk or electric hand mixer to break the ice crystals, creating a smooth consistency. Repeat this 3 or 4 times every 30 minutes, then store the gelato in a plastic tub with a well-fitting lid.

7. Remove the gelato from the freezer 10 minutes before serving.

Liquorice

Liquorice has been synonymous with the West Yorkshire town of Pontefract for nearly 400 years, brought from the Mediterranean by Dominican monks in the early 16th century. The Pontefract area provides excellent growing conditions for the liquorice plant due to the deep soil enriched by local muck. However, the 20th century saw the plant's cultivation all but cease because of cheaper imports. The plant, however, is now homegrown once more with local farmer Robert Copley having planted half an acre, which will hardly supply the sweet industry, but is a start.

Originally, the liquorice was used purely for medicinal purposes in the form of a small cake or pomfret invented by George Saville. In 1760 apothecary George Dunhill added sugar to the cake, and thus the liquorice sweet was born. The sweets continued to be made by hand in Pontefract until the 1960s, where experienced workers, commonly known as 'thumpers', used their hands to make the cakes and were able to stamp out 30,000 cakes a day. Now, they are machine-made.

One of the most popular uses of liquorice in sweets is the Allsort. Who does not know or recognise Bertie, the Allsort boy who is possibly one of the world's most recognised confectionery brands. Cadbury now own Bassett's, but their roots are from Sheffield where the company was formed by George Bassett in 1842 and then went on to produce Liquorice Novelties, a combination of liquorice and cream paste.

The myth goes that, in 1899, Bassett's salesman, Charlie Thompson clumsily gathered his sample boxes of novelties together and knocked them over and spilling the colourful sweets in the jumble of the counter, accidentally gave birth to the Allsort, which remains as popular and virtually unchanged today.

Liquorice Ice Cream

serves 6

140 g soft black liquorice
200 ml water
200 ml full-fat milk
300 ml double cream
1 teaspoon vanilla bean paste or 2 teaspoons extract
4 large egg yolks
50 g caster sugar

1. Start by finely chopping 115 g of the liquorice and put it in a small saucepan, add the water and bring to a gentle boil. Stirring often, cook until the liquorice has melted, and you have a thick dark paste. Remove from the heat.

2. Heat the milk, cream, and vanilla in another saucepan, again to a gentle simmer, then immediately remove from the heat and put to one side to infuse.

3. Using either a hand whisk or stand mixer, whisk the egg yolks and sugar together until light and creamy. Still whisking, add the infused cream and milk, then return the mixture to the saucepan. Over low heat and while stirring continuously, cook until the custard starts to thicken. Do not boil as this will curdle the milk. Pour the custard into the melted liquorice and stir, then pass through a fine sieve into a jug.

4. Finely chop the remaining liquorice into tiny pieces and stir into the custard. Lay a piece of clingfilm onto the surface of the custard, leave to cool and put into the fridge to chill right down, this will take at least an hour.

In an ice cream machine: churn following the manufacturer's instructions. Put the ice cream into a freezer box, cover it with a lid, and pop it in the freezer. The liquorice ice cream will keep for up to one month.

Without an ice cream machine: put the cooled custard into the freezer for 30 minutes. Take it out and beat with either a fork, hand whisk or electric hand mixer to break the ice crystals, creating a smooth consistency. Repeat this 3 or 4 times every 30 minutes, then store the ice cream in a plastic tub with a well-fitting lid.

Remove the ice cream from the freezer 10 minutes before serving.

Raspberry and Skyr Yoghurt Lollies

When Hesper Farm near Skipton launched their Skyr, they were the first in Britain to make the thick, creamy, super-healthy – thanks to being high in protein and naturally non-fat – Icelandic yoghurt.

Sam, son of farmers Brian and Judith, at just 21 years old, started the journey to make Skyr in Reykjavik, where Sam met skyr-master and mentor Thorarinn, who taught Sam the ancient art of making Skyr. And this is how they continue to make it in the Yorkshire Dales today.

When I first tasted their flavoured Skyr (cold brew coffee and vanilla is my favourite), I started making ice cream with it, not too successfully, but when I tried it as ice lollies for the children, it was a dream to use and a lovely texture.

makes 6 – depending on the size of the mould

125 g fresh raspberries
55 g caster sugar
2 tablespoons cold water
300 ml natural Skyr yoghurt

1 teaspoon vanilla extract
65 g 60% chocolate, finely grated
115 g mixed nuts, finely chopped

1. Place the raspberries and sugar into a small saucepan, add the water and cook over low heat until the raspberries start to release their juices and soften. Remove the raspberries from the heat and put them to one side to cool slightly before pressing through a fine sieve to separate the pulp and the seeds.

2. Using a hand blender, blend the Skyr yoghurt with the pulp and the vanilla extract to create a smooth, creamy mixture. Pour the cream into silicone lolly moulds and tap the mould firmly on the worktop to release any trapped air bubbles. Insert a lolly stick, and pop them into the freezer for a couple of hours, depending on the size of the lollies.

3. Once the lollies are frozen, put grated chocolate into a small heatproof bowl. Over a pan of simmering water, making sure the bowl does not touch the water, stir with a wooden spoon until melted. Put the chopped nuts into another bowl.

4. Half dip each lolly into the chocolate, then into the nuts and get them back into the freezer as quickly as possible. Once the chocolate sets, store the lollies in a plastic box in the freezer to keep them fresh and prevent cross-smells from other foods. Eat within a month – if you can resist them that long.

Danish Risalamande
– Danish Christmas Pudding

Having spent several happy Christmases when living in France, I would usually cook and serve traditional French festive foods, although occasionally I would long for a bit of good British custom with goose or turkey, pigs in blankets, Christmas pudding and so on. And, as my then partner was Danish, we would of course add in a little Danish too; it was an eclectic mix but great fun.

The favourite Christmas tradition from Denmark I would make for the children was this delicious variation of rice pudding. In addition to stewed apple there's whipped cream, chopped almonds, and importantly one whole almond. Whoever finds the much-prized whole almond in their dessert wins a prize which traditionally is a marzipan pig, but any small prize would do.

The children especially loved this game and would fall silent as they carefully ate their way through the dessert, taking care not to bite into the whole almond, which if they did, meant no prize.

serves 4

1 large vanilla pod	1 tablespoon water
½ litre full-fat milk	2 tablespoons sugar
100 g short-grain pudding rice	50 g skinned almonds, chopped
2 Bramley cooking apples	plus 1 whole
1 tablespoon honey, optional	400 ml whipping cream

1. Split the vanilla pod in two and scrape out the seeds with the blade of a small knife.

2. Bring the milk to a boil, add the vanilla pod and seeds, the rice, and then stir gently. Lower the heat and simmer for about 50 minutes, stirring from time to time. When ready, the rice should be creamy but not too wet; if it is, cook a little longer. Remove the vanilla pod and leave it to cool completely. You can do this step the day before if you wish.

3. Meanwhile, peel and core the apples, chop roughly into bite-sized chunks and cook with the honey (if using) and a tablespoon of water until the apples have broken down and are fluffy in texture. Leave to cool.

4. Stir the apple, sugar and chopped almonds into the cold rice. Then, whip the cream until fairly stiff and fold carefully into the rice mixture. Add the whole almond and stir gently.

5. Serve at once in your prettiest bowls or glasses.

Tuscan Sunshine and Tomato Sauce

I found this recipe in an old cookbook when running my cookery classes at the 12th-century Villa Catureglio, high in the hills north of Lucca. I was captivated by the unusual cooking method where they insisted on no stirring whatsoever and were exacting in the careful cutting of the soffritto – the carrots, onion, celery and garlic for the base flavour of the sauce. All the vegetables must be tiny for the best possible taste and are layered meticulously in a set order into the cooking pan. Finally, this is topped off with fresh skinned and deseeded tomatoes, handfuls of fresh basil, parsley and glugs of peppery Tuscan olive oil. The cooking was long and slow over several hours, and with a no-stirring clause, the ingredients gently melt together to create the finished sauce. I followed this method of making the sauce faithfully, and it indeed was sensational.

Making the sauce that way was wonderful, but back in Yorkshire and eventually with a family to feed every day, I worked on the recipe to make it more practical for me, and I am happy with the results. I use my food processor to chop the vegetables and make the sauce in my Sage pressure cooker with the sauce cooked and ready in under an hour, but you can make it easily in a large pan or stock pot. The sauce still has its intense depth of flavour, and the only missing ingredient is the Tuscan sunshine.

The sauce's versatility is incredible; over pasta, it will beat any jar you can buy; so tasty for a homemade pizza; turn it into the best tomato soup (below) or the showstopper of a dish, the Tuscan tomato tart on page 144.

The recipe makes approximately 1 litre of sauce

8 tablespoons extra virgin olive oil
1 small onion, roughly chopped
2 medium or 1 large carrot, peeled and roughly chopped
1 celery stalk, roughly chopped
2 cloves garlic
small handful of flat-leaf parsley
small handful of basil leaves
2 x 400 g tins of chopped tomatoes
salt and pepper

1. Put 1 tablespoon of the oil, the onion, carrot, celery, garlic, parsley and basil into a food processor and blitz to chop them up small enough to cook quickly but not too much that they turn to a paste.

2. To make it by hand, finely slice the onions and garlic, chop the carrots and celery into tiny cubes, and roughly chop the parsley and basil.

3. Heat 2 tablespoons of olive oil in a large saucepan or stockpot, add the chopped vegetables and cook gently to soften for about 15 minutes.

4. Add the tinned tomatoes, including the juice, pour the remaining olive oil over and bring to a gentle boil, turn the heat down and cook uncovered until the vegetables are tender and have broken down into the tomatoes. Be warned; this can be a messy business because cooked on too high heat will splatter everywhere. Keep an eye on the sauce to make sure it is not sticking, by either giving the sauce a good shake, or a quick stir. Aim for a thick, well-reduced sauce, which can take up to an hour and perhaps a little longer depending on how small you chopped the veg.

5. Taste and season the sauce with a bit of salt and pepper. The sauce is now ready to use. If not using immediately, cool and keep it covered in the fridge, or it freezes very well and keeps for up to 3 months.

One Sauce – Five Recipes

1. The sauce can be used over any pasta or gnocchi and layered up in a lasagne. If you over-reduce the sauce, it is very forgiving, and by adding in a little boiling water and stirring through, it will loosen up again. Or, if you feel generous, a good slug of olive oil.

2. Take your homemade pizza to another level with this sauce as your base. As it is very rich, do not overload onto the base, a little will go a long way.

3. For a thick, creamy soup, put 500 g of the sauce into a saucepan and add 500 ml of vegetable or chicken stock. Bring to a gentle simmer for five minutes. Tip into a food processor, add 50 ml double cream and blitz. Season to taste and add more cream to your liking, another quick blitz, then serve at once or reduce further for a thicker soup.

4. Blend the thick sauce to create a silky smoother version which is lovely spooned over steamed fish. Or, add a few chilli flakes for a bit of heat and super with grilled meats.

5. Don't forget the tomato tart recipe on (page 144).

Shortcrust Pastry

Seriously, there is no need to fear making shortcrust pastry. There are those who make out it is difficult, but I have no idea why. Shortcrust pastry is merely flour, fat, cold water and perhaps a pinch of salt or a little sugar. That is it.

Read the hints and tips below if you are new to making the pastry. Otherwise, crack on with this recipe. I have been using it for years, and it rarely lets me down.

My shortcrust pastry

This recipe makes 300 g of pastry, enough for a regular-sized pie or flan, or at least 12 jam tarts or mince pies. See the pastry calculator below for different quantities.

200 g plain flour
110 g butter or a 50/50 mix of butter and lard
pinch of salt
2 tablespoons cold water

Now is the time to choose – by hand or machine?

It is up to you, but I often use a food processor or my Thermomix. A machine makes short work of the pastry and prevents the mixture from getting too hot. The only danger in using a machine is if you overmix, this will warm the mix and make it too crumbly to bind together.

Hand-making, though, is lovely if you have the time; apply a light touch and keep your hands, bowl and ingredients as cold as you possibly can.

By hand:

1. Using a large, clean, cold mixing bowl, sift in the flour, then add the butter and salt. Gently rub the mixture between your fingers to incorporate the fat into the flour, lifting as you rub to add a little air for a light pastry until the mix resembles fine breadcrumbs.

2. Add the cold water a little at a time, and using a cold knife, stir to bind the dough together. Do not over mix. Add more water as needed.

3. Wrap the dough in clingfilm and chill for at least 15 minutes, longer if you can.

By machine:

1. Place the flour, butter and salt into the bowl of the processor.

2. Pulse until the mixture resembles breadcrumbs as above; this will happen quickly. With the motor running, add the water a little at a time, and the instant the pastry starts to bind, stop the motor.

3. Tip the pastry onto the work surface, lightly bring it together, and wrap in cling as above.

That is all there is to it because once the pastry has rested, it is ready to use in all your favourite recipes.

Rich, sweet pastry aka pâte sucrée:

Sometimes a sweeter, stronger pastry is needed, especially for desserts and sweet pies, as it adds extra flavour and depth. A sweet pastry recipe is similar to basic shortcrust but is all butter and has egg as a binder plus sugar.

200 g plain flour
110 g butter
25 g caster sugar
1 medium free-range egg, lightly beaten
splash of milk to bind if needed

1. Place all the ingredients except the egg and milk into either a large baking bowl or a food processor. Rub the fats into the flour with your fingertips until the mixture resembles breadcrumbs or if using a food processor, repeatedly pulse until like breadcrumbs.

2. Add the beaten egg and mix with a knife or pulse setting to bind the pastry together; if the pastry isn't binding well, add a drop of milk and mix again; you need a firm but not sticky dough; if it is sticky, sparingly add a little more flour.

3.   Once bound, tip onto the worktop and gently knead to form a ball of dough, wrap in clingfilm, and rest in the fridge for at least 30 minutes.

If you find it challenging to roll out rich pastry, try rolling between two sheets of parchment or flour-dusted clingfilm.

Blind baking:

I rarely blind bake anything these days once I discovered the pizza setting on my oven, which uses a combination of the fan oven and the bottom heating element. The extra heat from below ensures your pasty cooks through while the filling gets a gentler heat. I find it perfect for quiche and other wet fillings. So, if you have a pizza setting, do give it a try.

How to blind bake:

1.   Roll out the pastry, large enough to line the base and sides with a little extra above the rim for trimming.

2.   Gently lift the pastry and, without stretching, loosely line the tin.

3.   Tear a piece of excess pastry, roll it into a small ball, and press the pastry into the corners and edges of the tin. Trim the top, then crimp using your thumb and index finger, then pop it into the fridge to rest for 30 minutes or longer, if you have the time.

4.   Preheat the oven to 200°C.

5.   Crumple a sheet of baking paper, large enough to cover the base and sides of your pastry then smooth it out, place it in the tart and fill with baking beans if you have them, or use rice if not (I keep a jar of rice which I use over and over). Cook for 10 minutes or until the edge starts to brown. Remove the paper and beans or rice and cook for 5 minutes more.

Simple pastry calculator

This table will help you roughly estimate what you can comfortably make with a given quantity of pastry. Adding the weight of flour and fat in the recipe will give you a rough idea of the pastry weight.

•   300 g pastry will line a 23 cm tin, or line and cover a 15 cm pie.

•   350 g pastry will line a 25 cm tin and line and cover an 18 cm pie.

•   450 g pastry will line a 30 cm tin or line and cover a 23 cm pie.

The Stock Pot

I am often asked why, when there are all kinds of stock cubes and bottled substitutes available on the market, would I even think about making stock; indeed, this is a task made useless now, surely? To me, though, using homemade stock in a soup or sauce adds a depth of flavour and builds character to the dish.

Shop-bought stocks have improved from what they once were, especially having a closer eye on salt and additives, and some of them are pretty good and come in handy to have in the cupboard.

A major part of making stock that I love is that I don't waste chicken carcasses, lamb or fish bones. They all get used as I wrap them up and freeze until I have sufficient to put the stockpot on.

Here are three of my favourite stock recipes and are all I ever need for cooking.

Dark chicken stock makes about 2 litres of stock

6 tablespoons vegetable oil
2 or 3 chicken carcasses broken into
    pieces
½ glass of red wine or a shot of
    cognac
1 large onion with skin on, halved
1 carrot peeled and roughly
    chopped

1 stalk of celery, chopped
½ leek, cleaned and sliced roughly
2 cloves of garlic, peeled
parsley including stalks
12 black peppercorns
2 bay leaves, fresh or dried

1.   Heat the oil to hot in a large stockpot and add the chicken bones and brown, stirring constantly. Remove the bones and keep them to one side.

2.   Pour off any excess oil, place the pan back on a high heat and when smoking slightly, add the wine or cognac and scrape up all the juices and bits from the bottom of the pan.

3.   Reduce the heat slightly, place the onion cut side down in the juices and cook for 3 minutes to brown the onion slightly. Add the chopped carrot, celery, and leeks and stir around in the juices and onion for a few minutes. Then, add the garlic, parsley, peppercorns and bay leaves and stir. Add the bones back to the pan and cover with cold water.

4.   Bring to a boil, then reduce the heat and simmer for 2–3 hours, skimming often to remove scum and grease. Do not boil, as this will make the stock greasy and cloudy.

5.   After around 3 hours, remove from the heat and cool down rapidly. If possible, leave overnight in a cold place, and the next day remove any fat from the surface.

6. Strain, bring back to the boil and reduce to strengthen the flavour or reduce by two-thirds if freezing. Cool down and pack into small containers and freeze.

Vegetable Stock Makes around 1.5 litres of stock
Making this stock is so quick and straightforward that you will never reach for a cube again.

1 celery stalk, chopped
2 carrots, chopped
1 onion peeled and cut in half
a few parsley stalks

1 bay leaf
6 white peppercorns
good pinch of salt
2 litres of water

Add all the ingredients to the water in a large pan. Bring up to the boil and then simmer gently for 30 minutes. Strain and use in a favourite recipe.

Fish Stock Makes 1.5 litres

1 kg white fish bones (avoid using salmon as this is too greasy)
2 litres water
200 ml dry white wine
1 small onion, thinly sliced

a small handful of parsley, leaves and stalks
a few small white mushrooms, sliced
12 white peppercorns

Place all the ingredients in a stockpot. Bring to a boil, and then turn the heat down at once. Never boil a fish stock, or it will taste very bitter. Simmer gently for 20 minutes. Remove from the heat, strain and leave to cool. Freeze if not using straight away.

Kitchen notes on stock-making:

To make light chicken stock, omit the seared onion and replace it with a peeled, chopped onion.

Stock, when ready, must be cooled quickly by plunging the stockpot into a large sink or bucket filled with cold or iced water.

Never place a lid entirely on a cooling stock, as it will turn sour. Instead, leave a small space for the steam to escape.

Do not add salt to the stock unless the recipe asks for it as seasoning will usually happen when used in a recipe.

Duck Fat Chips

makes 4 good portions
900 g floury potatoes (Desiree, Estima, King Edward or Maris Piper)
500 g duck fat
Maldon salt (optional)

1. Peel the potatoes. Cut into generous 1.25 cm slices, then cut into roughly 1.25 cm chunky chips. Place the chips into a colander and rinse under cold running water until the water runs clear.

2. Bring a large pot of water to a boil, add the chips and cook for 4 minutes. Drain, then spread them onto either a clean kitchen towel or paper. Pat to dry thoroughly and leave to go cold.

3. Before cooking the chips, line a large roasting tin with a paper towel and have a slotted spoon to hand.

4. In a large pot, melt the duck fat and heat to 190°C (if you don't have a thermometer, the fat is hot enough when you drop in a chip and it sizzles and floats to the surface).

5. Put only enough chips into the hot fat to form a single layer; the temperature will drop once they are in, so turn the heat up slightly. Let them sizzle and rise back to the surface, then cook for 4–5 minutes until they are just starting to brown; stir with the slotted spoon from time to time. Finally, scoop them up and lay them onto the kitchen paper to drain and cool.

6. Wait for the fat temperature to rise again, add another layer and repeat. Continue until you have partially cooked them all. At this point, you can keep them to finish off when ready to serve by covering them with a tea cloth and popping the tray into the refrigerator.

7. Once you are ready to serve, reheat the fat and prepare another dish with a kitchen towel.

8. This time, you can add more chips than before, but not so many that the pan is crowded – fewer is better. They will crispen up and turn golden within minutes, so keep an eye on them and as soon as they look like they are going from golden to dark, whip them out, drain on the paper, then keep warm until you have cooked the rest.

9. Serve immediately sprinkled with salt if you prefer. Enjoy.

Homemade Pickled Onions

No self-respecting pork pie or ploughman's would ever be seen without a delicious fat, lightly spiced pickled onion. I for one love them, especially with a pork pie.

Making them takes time and it can be a little tedious, but the results are so, so worth it. Buy the onions in late autumn, early winter, get cracking with them and you will be serving them on Boxing Day.

1 kg pickling onions
25 g salt
for pickling:
½ teaspoon coriander seeds
½ teaspoon mustard seeds
½ teaspoon black peppercorns
½ teaspoon dried chilli flakes
1 litre malt vinegar
170 g sugar

1.   Top and tail the onions then place them in a large heatproof bowl and pour boiling water over to cover. Leave to cool, and once the water is cool, hey presto, the skins will just rub away.

2.   Once you have rubbed the skins away, pat the onions dry with a kitchen towel.

3.   Sprinkle the salt over the dry, peeled onions. Stir to make sure the salt is distributed and leave overnight. (Do not leave longer than overnight if you want your onions to be crisp.)

4.   When ready, rinse the onions and dry with kitchen towel.

5.   Mix together the pickling spices.

6.   Place the spices, vinegar, and sugar into a large stainless-steel pan.

7.   Heat to dissolve the sugar, but do not boil.

8.   Pack the onions into clean, sterilised jars.

9.   Pour the vinegar and spice liquid over to fill the jars, making sure each jar has pickling spices in it and that there are no air pockets.

10. Seal the jars and leave to cool. The onions will be ready to eat after about one month, though they will be better if kept for two.

Homemade Pesto

55 g coarsely chopped fresh basil leaves
½ clove garlic, crushed
150 ml extra virgin olive oil
1 tablespoon freshly grated pecorino Romano cheese
1 tablespoon freshly grated Parmesan cheese
1 tablespoon pine nuts
tiny pinch of sea salt

1. Put the basil leaves and crushed garlic clove into a food processor and pulse to combine. With the processor blades still running, slowly add the olive oil in a continuous drizzle until combined with the basil.

2. Add both the cheeses and pine nuts and then blitz again just a couple of times; too much, and the leaves may be over-chopped and can become bitter. Only add salt if you think you need it; there's a lot of cheese in there. Store the dressing in a screw-top jar; it will keep for up to 2 weeks.

Cooling Cucumber Raita

Cucumber raita is a delicious cooling agent for spicy foods. Though cooling may be the intention of raita, it is also perfectly delicious, served alone or with flatbreads or pitta bread.

Often raita is called a condiment, but it is quite different from condiments such as ketchup or mustard and usually served to cool or contrast the hot spices in curries and kebabs or as a dip.

Many seasonings can go into raita depending on the recipe or the region it comes from, including roasted cumin seeds, mint, chaat masala, or coriander.

serves 4–6

1 large cucumber
2 teaspoons sea salt
250 ml thick Greek yoghurt

1 large sprig fresh mint, chopped
1 pinch freshly ground black pepper
1 squeeze lime juice

1. Peel and grate the cucumber into a bowl. Sprinkle with the salt and stir. Leave to stand for 10 minutes for the salt to draw out excess water from the cucumber.

2. Place the grated cucumber into a sieve over a small bowl. Press gently with the back of a tablespoon to squeeze out any remaining moisture. Be careful not to press too hard, or you risk mashing the flesh of the cucumber into a pulp – it needs to remain firm.

3. Put the yoghurt into a bowl, add the mint and pepper and stir. Add the drained cucumber and stir again.

4. Finally, add the lime juice and serve. If not using immediately, cover with clingfilm and keep in the fridge where it will keep well for a couple of days.

Super Easy Hasselback Potatoes

Hasselback potatoes are so easy to make and look stunning on the plate. They have true versatility in the kitchen as you can change out the herbs you use; top them with grated cheese for a standalone meal and they are delicious alongside a Sunday roast too.

This style of cooking potatoes comes from Sweden specifically, the Stockholm's Hasselbacken Hotel in Stockholm.

serves 4

4 tablespoons extra virgin olive oil
1 clove garlic, peeled and very lightly crushed
3 sage leaves, or herb of your choice
4 Maris Piper (or other roasting or baking potato)
Maldon salt

1. Heat the oven to 200°C.

2. Gently heat the oil in a saucepan, add the garlic, sage or your chosen herb. Lower the heat and leave to infuse the flavours into the oil.

3. One at a time, place the potatoes onto a wooden spoon and cut three-quarters of the way down through the potato to create thick slices, taking care not to cut all the way through. The wooden spoon will help to avoid this.

4. Pop the potatoes into a roasting tin or ovenproof baking dish. Pour over the oil, ensuring it goes deep into the cuts, sprinkle generously with salt and bake for 50–60 minutes or until the potatoes are tender when pricked with a skewer or point of a knife.

5. Serve at once for the best flavour and texture or cover and keep warm until needed.

Suppliers

These are just a few of my favourites here in Yorkshire. Of course, there are hundreds more, but I use all of these, so they come with my tried and tested recommendation and most of them have been part of the Yorkshire food scene for a long time.

Meat, game and poultry

David Lishman – award-winning meats and charcuterie
Lishman's of Ilkley, 25 Leeds Road, Ilkley, West Yorkshire, LS29 8DP
01943 609436

Town End Farm Shop – meat, charcuterie and bags more
Airton, Skipton, BD23 4BE
01729 830902

Herb Fed Poultry – fabulous chicken and turkey
Shires Farm, York Road, Easingwold, North Yorkshire, YO61 3EH
01347 823155

Farmison & Co – free-range, sustainable meat and poultry
Bondgate Green, Ripon, North Yorkshire, HG4 1QW
01765 824050

Fish, seafood and smokeries

Cross of York
3 Market Street, York, YO1 7LA
01904 627590

R Bethell
321 Kirkgate Market, Leeds, LS2 7HN
0113 243 2810

Staal Smokehouse
Riston Road, Long Riston, Hull, HU11 5SA
01964 541946

Fortune's Kippers
22 Henrietta St, Whitby, YO22 4DW
01947 601659

Dairy and eggs

Yorkshire is awash with fabulous cheesemakers, the more-famous such as Wensleydale Creamery and Shepherds Purse are available to buy across the UK. For artisan cheeses check out the following.
Courtyard Dairy – national and international award-winning cheesemonger
Crows Nest Farm, near Settle, Austwick, LA2 8AS
01729 823291
or
Love Cheese
16 Gillygate, York, YO31 7EQ
01904 622967

Eggs
Yolk Farm and Minskip Farm shop –
home to happy hens and gorgeous
eggs and an "egg restaurant"
Minskip Road, Minskip, near
Boroughbridge, YO51 9HY
01423 329063

Yoghurt
*Hesper – Yorkshire's famous skyr
producers*
(the skyr can now be bought in farm
shops, delis and good supermarkets)
Hesper Farm Dairy, Bell Busk, Skipton

Larder

Herbs and spices
Herbs Unlimited – fabulous herbs
which can be bought in good
greengrocers, food halls and farm
shops
Sand Hutton Growers, Busby Stoop
Road, Sand Hutton, YO7 4RN

Rafi's Spice Box
17 Goodramgate, York, YO1 7LW
01904 430850

Saffron Tree
Follifoot Ridge Business Park, 4c
Pannal Road, Harrogate, HG3 1DP
01423 871767

Steenbergs – organic herbs and spices
6 Hallikeld Close, Melmerby, Ripon,
HG4 5GZ

Dry goods
Yorkshire Pasta – artisan British pasta
made in Yorkshire
For a list of stockists see their website
yorkshirepasta.co.uk

Yorkshire Organic Millers – flour grown
and milled in Yorkshire
For stockists see their website
yorkshireorganicmillers.com

Stocks
For chef-quality ready made stocks
Truefoods in Ripon.
truefoodsltd.com

Using the wealth of farm shops, delis,
food halls and grocers, you can find
bags more Yorkshire produce.

Just a few of my favourites:
*Lewis and Cooper Grocers,
Northallerton; Fodder Farm Shop,
Harrogate; Farmer Copleys Farm
Shop, Pontefract; Keelham Farm
Shop, Skipton; Drewtons Farm Shop,
South Cave; Cannon Hall Farm Shop,
Barnsley.*

For more information on fabulous
food in Yorkshire, take a look at or
contact Deliciously Yorkshire at
deliciouslyyorkshire.co.uk

Kitchen equipment
You will be hard pushed to find a
more comprehensive supplier of
all things cooking and home than
Lakeland. Though not a Yorkshire
company, they have shops in the
county and online.
lakeland.co.uk

RECIPE INDEX

Acknowledgements

My first thanks must be to David Burrill and Roger Arnold for taking me up on my book proposal, which, thanks to various life's challenges, not least the Covid pandemic, have meant delays and ultimately a change of direction. As always, their support and advice have been invaluable, and David's patience with me is remarkable, thank you.

So many friends, family and people along the way have had a part to play in the book, but I must say a huge thank you to Lucy, an awesome recipe tester and wonderful stepdaughter. And to my lovely bestest friend and often partner in fabulous adventures, Yvonne. She has patiently worked through all the recipes, reading, making the first edit and tons of advice and suggestions. Thank you, and love you always. Thanks too to Ernie for generously supporting Yvonne and me in all we have done together over the years.

Mum and Dad, what can I say? I love and miss you every day; my thanks to you are immeasurable.

So many friends, in so many ways, have supported me through different parts of my life. To those who have stood the course of time, Mandi, Wendy, Lena and Bengt, Jayne and Paul; all my lovely brothers and sisters and their families too, my life could never have been so wonderful without you all in it.

Immense thanks to my three stepchildren and their partners for the joys and occasional challenges along the way. And for bringing my absolute loves, Harry, Peggy and Frank, into my life.

None of this would have been possible without by my side my gorgeous husband. My fiercest love and kindest critic. Thank you. There is no better hand to hold as we walk through life together.

Finally, thank you to all the Yorkshire producers, farmers, growers, chefs, restaurateurs, retailers, and others for making Yorkshire the rich, diverse, magical place it is.

Elaine Lemm – June 2022

… the story continues.